Secrets of a Fulfilled Woman

Secrets
of a
Fulfilled
Woman

Finding True Contentment in Your Life

Barbara Peretti • Nancy Missler
Bonnie Thomas • Rexella Van Impe
Barbara Barker • Dottie McDowell
Darlene Ankerberg • Elizabeth Newbold
Compiled by Susie Perkins

New Leaf Press

First printing: September 1997
Second printing: November 1997
Third printing: December 2000

ISBN: 0-89221-367-1
Library of Congress Catalog Number: 97-68956

Cover by Steve Diggs & Friends, Nashville, TN

Printed in the United States of America.

Please visit our website for other great titles:
www.newleafpress.net

For information regarding publicity for author interviews contact Dianna Fletcher at (870) 438-5288.

*For my daughters
Jamie and Taylor,
with love.*

*Look carefully at what your Father has
done in the lives of these women. I pray that
both of you will love Him just as much and
find Him just as faithful.*

Table of Contents

Susie Perkins

After graduating from Auburn University in 1975, Susie married Bill Perkins, who is now the executive director of Compass International, a non-profit Christian ministry. They have two home-schooled daughters, ages 12 and 6, and a beagle named Sheckles.

Susie has been a Christian for almost 20 years and is a freelance writer and editor who has published a number of essays and articles in Christian publications. Although she remains a "southerner" at heart, she currently lives in Coeur d'Alene, Idaho, where her husband's ministry is based.

Foreword

One of the things that so commends Christianity is that, throughout history, it doesn't tell us about many great and powerful people. More often than not, it tells only the stories of ordinary people who live great and powerful lives; and that because of Jesus Christ living through them.

This book is the story of eight women and how they have loved God, and been loved by Him, through all kinds of good and hard places. Their lives are a letter written to each one of us, much as Paul said of the Corinthians:

> You are a letter of Christ, cared for by us, written not with ink, but with the Spirit of the living God, not on tablets of stone, but on tablets of human hearts (2 Cor. 3:3).

There is much to be learned from the life stories of these women, many things about them, but far more about Him. And that's the real purpose of this book. Through their willingness to share their lives, they encourage us immensely and show us once again what great things God can do when we give Him a heart that is willing.

— Susie Perkins

Barbara Peretti

Barbara is the wife of best-selling author Frank Peretti, whose works include *This Present Darkness, Piercing the Darkness,* and *The Oath.* She is currently becoming an author in her own right, as she is completing an inspirational book based on her life story. The Perettis have settled in the mountains of the Pacific Northwest where they lend their time and efforts to a number of different ministries.

Chapter 1

"To Barbara Jean, wife and friend, who loved me and waited."

Dedication from Frank Peretti's
book, *This Present Darkness*

My husband, Frank, will tell you that the first thing he ever knew about girls at Bethel Church was that they wore yarn in their hair. At least, that's the report he'd gotten from his best friend, who always made it his mission to check out the girls.

I don't know how Frank felt at that time about girls with yarn in their hair, but since Bethel seemed to be one of the most solid evangelical, Bible-teaching churches on our little island in Puget Sound, he and his family ended up attending there along with me and my family. Frank found out firsthand that the girls in that church did, indeed, wear yarn in their hair . . . me included. I don't know, maybe it was the yarn in my hair that reached out and drew him. Anyway, this is where we first met.

Above All, Home

My family moved to Vashon Island near Seattle from our home in Idaho in 1969. Since we didn't have any extended family in the Northwest, the church became our family. We'd always been a church-going family for as long as I can remember, involved in things like vacation Bible school, family camps, choir, and youth group.

Before moving to Vashon we attended a Baptist church in Coeur d'Alene, Idaho. One Sunday evening service when I was

11

about eight or ten, the pastor gave an altar call to go forward and receive Jesus as Savior. I remember sitting next to my mom, leaning toward her, and asking, "Would you go forward with me?" She quietly took my hand and together we walked to the front of the church. That night I gave my heart to Jesus.

Thinking back, I now realize how very fortunate my brothers and sisters and I were, being raised in a Christian home that practiced godly principles. My father owned several dry cleaning and laundry businesses in town which kept him pretty busy. He always tried to keep his customers happy even though his job was pretty tough, toiling all day amid the hot, steaming machinery. He was well-liked, even voted by the Chamber of Commerce as "Man of the Year." But above and beyond all that, what I really remember is him coming home each night with that huge smile on his face, sweeping us kids into his arms, and smothering us in hugs and kisses. What a picture he portrayed for us of the loving Heavenly Father we learned about each Sunday! Then there was Mom, the personification of motherhood, although she'd deny that statement! She was always home for us with some delicious after-school snack, as dependable as the sun coming up each morning. Some nights she'd put us to bed after measuring a hem and we girls would wake the next morning to a new dress awaiting us. Often in our discussions Mom would open her Bible and say, "I was just reading about that . . . now where was it?" and proceed to read what the Bible had to say about our particular topic. We didn't have the privilege of attending a Christian school but we did get a continuous Christian education at home.

Our parents put so much of themselves into our lives. Today when we get together, we still talk about all the fun things we did growing up and all the places we went as a family.

Asking God

As a little girl, I'd sit (for what felt to me like hours) thinking about God and praying, wondering what it must be like to be close to Him. When I was in grade school I would take long walks (when that was still a safe thing to do) and the Lord and I would discuss all kinds of things. I was pretty open about my faith so most of the kids at school knew I was a Christian. I didn't consider myself as belonging to the "in crowd" but that didn't bother me. My walk with the Lord was most important. In junior high I prayed He'd help me make the cheerleading squad so I could be a witness for Him. He did and I got to cheer, so to keep my word, every chance I got I wouldn't hesitate to let people know I was a Christian. I remember asking the Lord questions about who I was supposed to date and things like that, which was a pretty big thing for a girl in seventh and eighth grade!

Even at 15 I didn't really see myself as a "normal" dating person. I was already thinking about marriage and becoming a homemaker. The life my mother had modeled before me was one I wanted for myself. I was never interested in attending college; my career was going to be a homemaker. I didn't consider that a lesser position in life for a woman, but as a very important position. I took it quite seriously and planned to give my all making a godly, happy home for myself and my husband, whoever he was to be. I put that part of the equation into God's hands.

It Took Me a While . . .

My first recollection of the Peretti family was meeting Frank's younger brother in Sunday school on Vashon Island. I remember thinking he was pretty good-looking and wondered where he'd come from. Not too long after that, Frank began coming to church. He and a friend sang a song together one evening at church and my father invited them to the house afterward. It took me a while to like Frank, actually. He, too, was good-looking but I thought he was just a little stuck on himself and definitely too skinny, weighing in at about 115 pounds. At first Frank thought I was just a "dippy little high school girl" giggling at everything. My giggling was so evident his mother started calling me "Bubbles." Well, at least I wasn't grumpy!

Without fully intending it to happen, Frank and I found ourselves as leaders of the church youth group. He'd already graduated from high school and started teaching Bible studies. Everyone liked him and I had to admit, even though he did seem stuck on himself, he had a lot of wisdom. We spent a great deal of time together working on various projects all through the winter.

Spring arrived and along with it opportunities for car washes to raise money for the youth group. In a surprise visit, a football player from Coeur d'Alene I'd spent two years dating showed up at a car wash ready to spend Easter weekend with my family. At the time, Frank would have told you that he certainly had no romantic inclinations toward me; however, he couldn't figure out why he was so upset because this guy had driven all the way from Idaho just to ruin our car wash!

Counselor and Friend

It is rather ironic that after Frank met my boyfriend he started counseling me about how to be a good girlfriend. Our transportation back then was the Peretti's 1949 Dodge Powerwagon, fondly named Tinkerbelle. It was in the cab of old Tinkerbelle that Frank lectured me on the merits of being a good girlfriend. All the while, I was learning more and more about Frank Peretti, liking what I was seeing!

Frank told me that to build a solid relationship you needed to give it your all. I remember him saying, "When somebody asks you to do something, you give them steak, not hamburger," referring to the quality of the relationship. He also talked of keeping oneself pure in the relationship and before the Lord.

Our work with the youth and the counseling sessions in Tinkerbelle were subtle ways the Lord was slowly bringing us together. We certainly didn't fall in love but rather grew in love over a period of several months.

Barbara Peretti

The Fleece

I had been following a "read through the Bible in a year" program, and one night while reading Deuteronomy 11, I felt the Lord speaking. The Scripture talked about God taking the Children of Israel out of the land from which they had come to a new land. He said this new land would have its mountains and valleys, that it would receive the early and the latter rain from His hand, and that He would multiply and provide for the needs of those whose hearts were committed to Him.

God was speaking to the Children of Israel, but that night it was as though He was speaking to me. In my life, the early rain represented the boy I had been dating, the latter rain represented Frank. The Lord seemed to be saying, "If you dedicate your life to me and follow me, I will give you the latter rain of your life. I will bless what you do and take care of you from the beginning of the year even to the end of the year."

For me, this was like leaving behind one life and moving on to a new life. I phoned Frank that night and read the Scripture to him asking if it meant anything to him. He didn't pick up on anything special. When we'd hung up, I did something I have never done at any other time in my life. I laid out a fleece before God: "Okay, Lord, if what you're telling me is what I think it is, if I'm supposed to leave my present boyfriend and marry Frank Peretti, then have Frank show up at school tomorrow."

Marrying Frank Peretti seemed really bizarre to me, and the idea of Frank showing up at school seemed almost equally bizarre, but that night, at 15 years of age, I left the question of who I was to marry in the Lord's hands.

The next day found me deep in study for an exam between periods in my history classroom. Suddenly a friend came flying into the room exclaiming, "Hey, Barb, guess who's here?" I honestly hadn't even thought of the night before so I was curious who the visitor was. "Frank Peretti's here!"

I felt a chill run from the top of my head to my feet. The

Holy Spirit descended upon me and tears welled up in my eyes. The full realization of what was happening hit me full force: my future husband stood on the other side of the wall! I didn't know how to act! I ran into the hall, grabbed Frank by the shoulders and asked, "WHAT ARE YOU DOING HERE?!"

Poor Frank, a bit confused by the commotion I'd started, didn't know the story behind the question and simply explained that the night before, a friend had asked him to come to the school and witness to a girl about Jesus. That's why he'd come. Frank's arrival changed two lives that day: my life was changed, and the girl he witnessed to accepted Jesus into her heart!

After Frank and I had been married several years, I heard a speaker at a seminar say, "You know, when God puts a mandate on your life, it makes all the difference, because you have a goal." I knew he was right. From that day in high school forward, I had a mandate: I was supposed to marry Frank Peretti.

Waiting for God's Timing

Frank and I probably knew each another eight months or so before we started actually dating. I had my mandate and two more years of schooling. I had to wait for God's timing.

Before meeting me, Frank had just broken up with a girl. They'd had a pretty intense romance and Frank wasn't ready to jump into another relationship too quickly. So at the end of our eight months of getting to know each other, Frank pretty much laid it on the line with me. "I'm concerned that we seem to be getting involved with each other. I feel I need to be honest with you. You are still young and need to know that I'm through dating. I'm seriously looking for my wife. If you are not interested in finding a husband we should put a stop to things now."

I think that Frank was pretty wise for his age as he continued, "I'm not going to hold your hand, I will not kiss you, hug you, nor put my arm around you until we decide that we are in love. Do you agree to that?" I did, I agreed.

For the next six or eight months, we spent time together checking each other out. Frank wanted to make sure that I was sold out to the Lord because he wanted to be really sold out to the Lord. Frank had thought these things through, and he wanted to just observe me and analyze my actions. He wanted assurance from the Lord that I was the one for him.

The whole time we dated we wrote notes back and forth to each other and always included the Lord in all we did. It was always Frank, Barb, and the Lord, a threesome. We prayed together a lot and it's pretty hard to do that without including the Lord!

We became best friends, doing everything together. Whatever it was, we wanted the other person there . . . it was just more fun that way! My relationship with the Lord deepened during that time because everything we did was as a threesome.

Commitment

There was an understanding between us that when Frank told me he loved me, it would mean that he wanted to marry me. On June 22, 1970, when I was 16 and Frank was 19, we were taking an evening walk and he asked me how I felt about him. I don't remember exactly what I said but I didn't come right out and tell him I was madly in love with him. I did leave him with some impression on a positive note. I did return the question to him, "How do *you* feel about *me*?" Well, he mumbled and fumbled around going through all kinds of crazy antics, throwing rocks and crushing the dirt under his feet. Ultimately, he ended up lying down in the middle of the road out of frustration. Gathering his thoughts along with himself, he stood and continued to walk. When we got to the bottom of his folks driveway he turned, looked me in the eye, and said, "I feel pretty strongly about you and have something I want to read to you." He tenderly reached over, drew me to him, and hugged me for the first time. We'd never touched each other, so this whole hugging idea was all new to us. Already feeling a bit awkward, we no sooner got our arms around each other than a neighbor came by walking his dog! We were so embarrassed about "getting caught" hugging each other, we dropped the idea and headed up the driveway to Frank's room.

Frank was pretty timid about this whole thing. After sitting down, with flashlight in hand he pulled his coat over his head and began reading from a note he'd pulled from his pocket. It was a love note, poetically written, declaring his feelings for me. We were in love! I was so touched. All I could fathom was that Frank was going to be my husband!

I still had my junior and senior high school years ahead of me so we decided we'd have to wait two more years. That night we set our wedding date for June 24, 1972, and that was the day we got married.

We kept our engagement secret until my 18th birthday when Frank gave me an engagement ring. Of course, by this time almost everyone knew we were in love, so it was not much of a surprise. A few years after we were married Frank's mother told us that when I was 15 and first walked into their house the Lord told her I was going to be Frank's wife. Being a wise mother, she withheld her knowledge until the appropriate time.

Making Ends Meet

Frank was playing banjo for a bluegrass group in Seattle when we were first engaged. He made ten dollars a night playing. The job lasted one weekend. After that, Frank got to know some people who had connections with a recording studio in Vancouver, Washington. The studio hired him as a backup musician, janitor, phone answerer, and general gopher. After we were married, we moved to a duplex in Vancouver. Frank was making $220.00 per month, rent was $123.75, our car payment was $50.00, and I had a weekly budget of $7.50 for groceries. We ate a lot of stuffed hot dogs and tuna dishes!

To help make ends meet, I found a job at a knitting mill

in Portland. It brought in a little extra income but I hated working. I used to cry before leaving the house some mornings because I really wanted to be home — that was my calling. I was raised in a home where Dad supported Mom and us kids and I wanted that same kind of situation. I was committed to our relationship, however, and was willing to pitch in if need be.

About six months into working at the studio, Frank lost his job. They couldn't afford him! Frank was determined to keep working and help get me home so he found a job driving a delivery truck for auto parts and was bringing home $400.00 per month. A raise! We found a trailer just outside of town to live in that would save us about $40.00 a month in rent. Our finances were looking better and I was able to leave the knitting mill and come home. We even had steak now and then! Our new home was located in a more rural, peaceful area which was something Frank and I really desired. He set up the second bedroom as his study and continued with a correspondence writing course he was working through.

While driving his delivery truck, Frank was offered a position as banjo player for a traveling family music show. We got to see many of America's beautiful sights, but after nine months of living paycheck-to-paycheck and calling a hotel room our "home," we left the group. We moved into my in-laws' basement for a year where Frank tried to start a business, building and repairing banjos as well as giving lessons. I returned to my high school job at a local greenhouse.

The Next Step

Frank and I traveled with a Christian music group and ministered for about two years in various churches up and down the northwest coast. After that, we worked various jobs for a year or so and then we both ended up working at a ski factory. Frank decided he wanted to attend film school at UCLA so we worked as much overtime as we could to make the move. Through a government grant and a work study program, Frank's schooling was pretty much paid for. I found an entry position with an insurance oriented company in Century City, so things were looking good.

But Los Angeles was such a huge, impersonal machine. We were attending a large mega-church where we didn't know anyone and never met the same people twice. It was really different from our church on Vashon of 40 to 50 people! Great spiritual teaching is one thing, but without the human touch, without warm Christian fellowship, a person can still starve spiritually. After about a year, we found a smaller, more intimate church where we felt at home, and God met our needs through the people there. To this day, we still have friends we met at that church.

Home Again

After two very difficult years living in Los Angeles while Frank attended his film classes, our whole plan was starting to fizzle. The film industry seemed to be a dog-eat-dog world which was something we had no interest in. About that time, Frank's dad called and invited Frank back to Vashon Island to help him pastor the small church we'd left. Frank had a few other offers at the same time. One was a potential writing position, another was an invitation to move to Hawaii and play banjo for another bluegrass group. All offers sounded good. We received some good advice from a friend who said, "Sometimes the Lord asks you, 'What do *you* want to do?' " Frank was pretty firm in his decision to quit dragging me all over the country pursuing dreams, so he gladly accepted his father's offer and we headed back home.

The church wasn't able to pay a full-time salary, so Frank worked in construction to help make ends meet. After a few years, the church paid Frank $750 a month and I eventually went back into insurance for a time. Finances were a bit slim but one of the benefits from our two years in Los Angeles was the chance to stash enough money into savings to make a down payment on a piece of property when we moved back to Vashon Island.

Barbara Peretti

Beginning in 1980, Frank and I spent several years preparing the land while living in an 8 by 24 foot travel trailer which sat on his folks' property about 200 feet north of our property line. On October 20, 1982, we moved the trailer to our own property, and Frank carried me over the property line. He smiled and said, "Well, Barbie, after ten years, welcome home!" I cried, he cried, we hugged, and for the first time we had a place we could call our own.

The Dark Days

We stayed in the pastorate about four years or so. Things went well for the first four years, but by the fifth year the stress of the ministry began to take its toll, and we began to suffer from "burnout." I call that time the "dark days" because it was the hardest time of our marriage. After all that we'd been through — the recording studio, the music groups, banjo making, Los Angeles — we were at the top of the ladder as far as the ministry is concerned and we were finding it wasn't what we wanted. In fact, we strongly felt it wasn't what *God* wanted for us either!

I found myself resentful of the church and tried to figure out why. I finally decided it was because the church was always taking my husband away and coming between us: calling him to meetings or asking him to teach a class or preach a sermon or lead worship. I rarely had the privilege of worshiping with my husband, an experience we used to enjoy and that bound us together with the Lord. It wasn't the Lord I was resentful of. As I wrote in my diary, "I'm not mad at God, I'm just sick of the *church*." Realizing we weren't "pastor" material, we finally stepped down from our position and a new pastor was hired. Recognizing the condition we were in, he took us aside and told us to get away for a while. He was our shepherd now and he wanted to see us healed.

Looking back, I can see that God used many of the experiences of those years for our good and for our instruction. The first three or four years, Frank was constantly teaching and preaching. Besides preaching in church, he spoke at camps, banquets, and youth rallies for all kinds of audiences. God was forging his speaking skills and it really was fruitful. My diary recounts us being gone 25 days out of one month because of engagements. I was trying to figure out why I felt so tired and depressed. We just couldn't continue as we'd been doing. We needed a rest.

When we were first married, we weren't sure what Frank's ultimate career would be. Maybe that was the Lord's blessing, for at the time only He knew all the struggles that lay ahead of us. But we were sure of this: we were in love and we had the Lord with us. I think that's what sustained us. We were young when we married, Frank 21, myself 18. With no promise of employment ahead I sure didn't marry him for his money! I married him because I admired him, he was my best friend, and I knew God had His hand on our life. I felt Frank was a wise man of God and I felt very secure in that fact.

"What Are We Supposed to Do, Lord?"

We always asked God for His guidance and direction in our life. "What is it we're supposed to be doing, Lord?" Neither of us wanted to launch a career unless God was behind it. It's as though the first years of our marriage were a proving time for us, almost our own wilderness wandering.

From childhood, Frank always had a burning desire to write, to tell a story. Throughout his school years he kept a journal of his life and always got high marks for his essays and stories. The call upon his life to become a writer never left him. He pursued his banjo playing, he even got his minister's license and held that position for five years, but writing has always been the driving force in his life.

So, our first 12 years of marriage taught us, tested us, honed us into the people God wanted us to be. That process still goes on today. God will always be honing us. We didn't realize it then, but through these experiences God gave us new and deeper insights into life, which in turn provided the foundation for the stories Frank would write.

After stepping down from the ministry, we were suddenly without an income and frustrated, not knowing where God wanted us. We cried out to Him, "God, where should we go, what should we do?" but God seemed not to answer. Frank was devastated by this time. The only option left for him to keep food on the table was to go back to work at the ski factory, and it was just like we'd come full circle. We'd worked in that factory back in 1976, wandered for seven years, and now, in 1983, we were back to zero again. Our spirits were sinking.

The only flicker of hope we had was a novel Frank had been working on during our years in the pastorate. We knew Frank had a gift for writing, but he'd never sold anything and we knew the chances of making a living as a writer were pretty slim. But still there was hope, a deep inner feeling that God had given Frank his ability and wanted him to use it.

We were still living in the trailer, but by 1984 or so we were finally able to build a plywood shack around the trailer, enlarging our living space so we could have a real bed. For four years we'd been sleeping on the trailer's dinette table, having to fold it up every morning in order to eat breakfast. It was a real frustrating time. We thought, *Is this all the Lord's going to do? Are we going to live in this trailer with a shack around it the rest of our lives?* I finally settled one thing in my own mind and recorded it in my journal: "All we can do is trust in the Lord because that's all we have left."

A passage of Scripture that really ministered to Frank and me during this time was John 6:66–68 where a number of Jesus' followers had left because His teaching was too hard for them to bear. After they left, Jesus turned to his closest disciples and said, "Are you going to leave me, too?" Peter answered, "Lord, to whom shall we go?" That's how Frank and I felt. We could have forsaken God's calling and involved ourselves in careers of our choosing, but deep down we both felt that out there somewhere in all that darkness there was *something;* we just didn't know what it was. It was a very dark time and yet, hidden somewhere deep in our souls, a spark of hope and faith still burned. We knew God would not leave us nor forsake us.

The darkness grew out of uncertainty. Frank was feeling like a failure as a husband, unable to provide for his wife. He'd tried so many things and now, at 33 years of age, he still didn't have a clear indication of what God wanted him to do. I remember Frank and I weeping because we'd tried so hard to serve the Lord and do the right thing. Frank had tried so hard to care for me, but nothing ever seemed to work out. I recall going to bed and feeling like a heavy weight was resting on my chest. All I could do was sigh to try to relieve the pressure. Fortunately, as a married couple, we loved the Lord and each other, so the problem didn't lie in our relationship. The problem was seeing no clear road before us and having to trust that one day a road would appear.

Frank and I had a few arguments during that time, but they never went unresolved. Frank would always lead in prayer, both of us crying but going off to bed reassured by God's Holy Spirit that all would be well.

"Just Write the Book!"

Well-meaning people kept asking us that painful question that was about as soothing as fingernails being scraped across a chalkboard, "What is Frank going to do? Will he go back to school? What is he planning next?" All he felt from the Lord was, "Write the book, just write the book." I'd come home from work anxious to spend the evening with Frank and he'd pull out the typewriter and start banging away. Sometimes I wanted to literally throw that thing out the door — until he started reading his manuscript to me. When I got a glimpse of what God was doing through him, I really got behind him. The darkness we were living in, our burned-out condition, our zero balance bank account, and Frank's wonderful manuscript were the ingredients God poured into my life that stirred up my desire to continually pray for our situation and Frank's project. I fasted about once a week for different lengths of time, taking long walks, sometimes twice a day, just to get alone and beseech the Lord, lifting up the book and Frank.

A turning point came when Frank worked up a series of talks for a youth camp. He told a serialized story in the morning chapel, then drew a spiritual lesson from the story in the evening chapel. The stories were so well-liked that the camp counselors and even the kids were suggesting Frank have them published in book form. Thinking that was a good idea, Frank put the first of his stories into written form and submitted it to several publishers. Eventually it was published as *The Door In The Dragon's Throat,* the first in the Cooper Kids Adventure Series, and the little book that "opened the door" to Frank's writing career. When our first box of books arrived with Frank's name on the cover it was as if the clouds of darkness that had surrounded us for so long were beginning to part. We could almost hear a choir of angels singing! We could finally see the road God had chosen for us.

About this same time, as Frank was helping a friend put a roof on his house, another story came to him. I remember him coming home, sitting at the typewriter, and pounding madly for several hours. In a matter of a few days he'd put together a radio drama he titled *Tilly.* He rounded up some friends from the church, hung blankets in the trailer to deaden the sound, set up a reel-to-reel tape recorder, and his first audio drama was born. With a cassette copy in hand, Frank went to KCIS, a local Christian radio station, and asked the program manager to listen to it. He was reluctant at first, claiming that radio dramas were a thing of the past. Finally, after further persuasion, he did listen to it and liked it well enough to air it on January 22, which was Right to Life Sunday. The program was re-broadcast several times and soon Focus On The Family had several copies floating around their offices. They decided to remake their own version. One day while Frank was working at the ski factory, above the din of about 100 portable radios tuned to various rock and roll stations, Frank heard the faint crackle of Dr. James Dobson's voice announcing their broadcast of Frank Peretti's audio drama *Tilly*.

What a picture! There stood Frank, one lone, little guy in the middle of a huge factory, wearing a blue denim work apron, safety glasses over his eyes and resin all over his tennis shoes, leaning in close to a cheap portable radio straining to hear his audio drama broadcast around the world for millions to hear! There was something very poetic about the moment.

Our life was picking up at a steady pace by now. Frank had signed a contract to write a series of stories for kids which became the Cooper Family Adventure Series. *Tilly* had been broadcast and a publisher was showing interest in it. We were both working and providing a steady income.

Celebration

Finally, on November 26, 1983, at 8:04 p.m., Frank put a period behind the last word of the last sentence to the novel he'd been writing for the past five years. It was a big moment. He turned to me and said, "Barb, it's done," and to celebrate we drove to our local Dairy Queen and I treated Frank to a banana split.

Money was still pretty tight! Frank received a five hundred dollar advance for his first kid's book, but there weren't any royalties stacking up in the bank at that time. We'd go into a Christian book store to browse and there, hidden among the *thousands* of books, down near the bottom of the children's section, way in the corner, we would find one familiar little book with only its spine showing. Not too impressive. It didn't really catch your eye or even jump out and say, "You gotta buy me!" No, there wasn't a lot of "buzz" about that first book!

Frank plugged away at the ski factory, I kept my job at the insurance agency, and slowly our financial situation began to take a turn for the better. It took us about six months to crawl out of debt, paying off bills and credit cards. We never had much money to get into debt with, but we did pay our income tax once with a credit card.

Assurance

About six months into Frank's employment at the ski factory, there were a couple of days when Frank really felt an intense presence of the Lord. It seemed to him as though the Lord was putting His hand on Frank's shoulder and saying, "All the dreams, all the desires of your heart, you will see. You will fulfill them; I'm going to help you fulfill them in the days ahead." The Lord gave Frank a deep assurance that all the years before had not been a mistake. God had led us the whole way, was still leading us, and knew what He was doing. While Frank stood there painting skis with tears rolling down his face, God seemed to open a little bit of the future to him and assured him that He was going to use him and all would work out in God's plan. Whenever Frank tells the story of those days, he starts crying. There's never been a moment like it since.

God has His own timing and for us the changes were gradual. Frank worked for two and a half more years before he could quit the ski factory. Even though *This Present Darkness* was finally accepted for publication, it still was not published until a year and a half later, and even then, the first year of sales was dismal. Frank's first royalty check came to a grand total of $127.00!

We were living in the same trailer with the same little shack around it, but we did graduate from an outhouse to an indoor toilet. So, as I said, things were gradually changing. My dream of having a *real* home had been on the back burner so long, it had boiled dry and was no longer an issue. I just gave it up to the Lord; I left it in His hands. The trailer with the shack around it was our home, such as it was, and I simply determined to make it comfy. We decorated it somewhat, kept it clean and warm, and arranged everything in its own place. Our little shack was always good to come home to, no matter what it was or what it looked like from the outside. It was ours and it was home.

Plodding now at a steady pace, everything seemed to be humming along smoothly. I think it was in 1987 that we got a call from the publisher. He was really excited because Frank's book had sold 4,000 copies that month. That was a big deal! We were excited! The next month it sold 10,000 copies, the month after that 30,000. In the months that followed, the sales just kept climbing as high as 50,0000 or 60,000 copies per month! It took off like a pea out of slingshot!

When You Need It . . .

As the months went by and the sales figures climbed, we began calculating royalties, planning to build a house. We decided to build with cash only and God gave Frank a slogan, "When you need it, it will be there." And so it was. We started with just enough money to hire a bulldozer to dig our basement and foundation. Then Frank and I grabbed shovels and for two years worked on the footings. Eventually, what grew out of that hole was a beautiful English Tudor home that God built with cash. It far exceeded our expectations; it was like a fairy tale.

It's funny to think about it now: we owned a large English Tudor home on three and a half acres with no mortgage, but when we applied for a Sears credit card they turned us down because we had no recent credit history! The greatest wisdom of man is still the foolishness of God!

The "Good Fail"

Had I not lived through it all, I wouldn't have the understanding I have now. I would not truly know with a knowledge which is *part* of me, that God is faithful. When you walk with the Lord and are obedient to His Word, if you apply His principles even when it's hard and do your best to fulfill everything you feel God has called you to do, then He'll be faithful to do as He promised. This is what Paul refers to as working out our salvation in fear and trembling. Building faith in God is like working out in a gym.

Lifting weights is hard, disciplined work that causes pain. It's the continual repair of the stressed tissue that builds the muscle. Weight lifters talk about "the good fail." They lift a weight until their muscle gives out, or "fails." Then they rest, letting the muscle repair itself. As a result, the muscle grows as it develops new layers of tissue. The process is hard and painful, but it produces results. Doesn't that sound like faith? It seems it's only when we're pushed to our limit that we finally call out to God in our need, seeking Him at last for His help and guidance. It's after our faith muscles have been pushed to their limit several times that we can look back and see the growth God has allowed in our lives.

The more we're tested, the stronger our faith becomes. When all is well, God gets a little of our attention, our prayers are few and short, God is our good friend. When we're in a time of testing, *all* our attention is focused on God, we're crying out and pleading for Him to not only be our good friend, but also our Savior, our protector, and our guide through our present situation. When we have nothing to rely on, no hope to rest in, no "big daddy" with a blank check to cover our needs, that's when God has our full attention. These can be the conditions that strengthen our faith.

God's Highest Calling

Not long ago, I was walking with my girlfriend. We were discussing the future economic picture of the nation. I told her how Frank and I had read publications and heard seminar speakers advising us to protect our assets through overseas investments, gold certificates, spreading one's portfolio through different stock acquisitions, and so on. She listened politely and then said, "That's really nice if you can do all that but all we can do is trust the Lord." I looked at her, she looked at me, and we both realized she'd said it all. That's exactly where we all need to be, trusting only in God. He's the supplier of all we need.

Secrets of a Fulfilled Woman

During our dark years, that's where Frank and I always were — depending solely on the Lord. Those were good faith-building years for us — worth their weight in gold! That's exactly where we need to be today. Though the bank account is looking better and the job is a little more secure, we still need to be depending solely upon our Lord, waiting on Him, waiting to hear His voice, waiting to follow His leading.

God has taught me so much about waiting on Him. So often we think we can do things on our own and often we can and do, but should we? Do we act too quickly before we've heard God's final instructions? Do we listen just to get the gist of the message, then run off and carry out only the part of His instructions we tarried long enough to hear? I think I married a smart and wise man. He could have launched many careers and done a lot of things. Out of desperation, we could have taken matters into our hands, gone off in a direction away from God's best for us, and really missed His highest calling. God has a plan and a time for us all and we can each find His best for us if we'll just slow down and wait. Be still and know that He is God.

My girlfriend tells me God called us to our present home to "live on the back side of the mountain." I believe she's right. He's put us in a position where we can be alone, shut out the world, get away, be quiet, and listen for His voice. It's slow here. We like it. We've found a peace and a rest where the waiting comes easy. We're at the end of a country road, tucked into a hill on the back side of the mountain. It's a good place where Frank and I and the Lord can still be a close threesome.

Nancy Missler

Nancy is an internationally known speaker and author of the King's High Way series of books and studies which include *The Way of Agape, Be Ye Transformed,* and *Why Should I Be the First to Change?* She is married to Chuck Missler, a dynamic former business executive whose books and Bible studies are distributed worldwide. Together, Chuck and Nancy founded Koinonia House, a publishing ministry that is designed to encourage and facilitate serious Bible study.

Chapter 2

When we were first married, Chuck used to say to me, "I can't promise you our marriage will be easy, but I do promise it won't be dull." He has kept that promise to the letter.

We were at 13,000 feet somewhere over the Colorado Rocky Mountains. The turbulence from the violent electrical storm tossed our small airplane, piloted by my husband, frantically back and forth across the dark gray sky. After what seemed like hours, we suddenly lurched to the right and headed straight downward, twisting, turning, and corkscrewing straight toward the ground. Both of our sons were with us, and the youngest one, Mark, was clinging to me as he sobbed. I have never in all my life been so petrified.

Sobbing, I cried out to God, "If You are really Lord and if You really do care and love me, then please, please save us from crashing, as I know in my heart that's what's going to happen. Lord, if You do save us, I promise to give You the rest of my life to do with whatever You will. Please, God, please."

It seemed like only a matter of seconds, certainly not more than a minute or two, and we pulled out from under that horrible and frightening storm. We crept along as close to the ground as we could, flying towards Colorado Springs where the control tower had said it was clear enough to land. Denver, it seemed, was still "locked in tight" with rain and fog. A few minutes later, we landed in Colorado Springs!

I will never forget this experience as long as I live. God

had truly heard my prayer and He had saved us. Now He was going to hold me to "my part" of the bargain. The next ten years of my life would prove to be the most difficult and painful ever, as God would lovingly "corner" me and make me faithful to do what I had promised Him that day in the plane.

Although I was definitely born again and God lived in my heart, up until that airplane incident in 1969 God had only been a part of my life. And He wasn't satisfied with that — He wanted more from me. He wanted the complete surrender of my life, so He could give me His own. Like the Israelites, I think God wanted me to understand the difference between just "entering the land" — which is asking Jesus Christ to come into our hearts and save us — and "possessing the land," which is something totally different. Possessing what we own is being so totally committed to Him, our wills and our lives, moment by moment, that we experience His Life through us.

I, personally, would never have chosen the ways God did over the next few years to bring me to that point of full surrender — possessing His land. In retrospect, however, after having passed through much of the fire, I can honestly say God's ways have been and are perfect for me.

"Whitewashed Tombs"

In the early 1970s, just after the airplane incident, if you had seen Chuck and me, on the outside we might have looked like a fairy-tale couple. We had been married almost 20 years and had four wonderful children, Chip, Mark, Lisa, and Michelle. Chuck had become a very highly successful business executive and we had a beautiful sprawling ranch house with a pool and stables.

But on the inside we were like so many people you see today: totally empty, unfulfilled, experiencing no real love, no meaning or purpose to our lives. We were what the Bible calls "whitewashed tombs," which look beautiful on the outside, but on the inside are full of dead men's bones.

Nancy Missler

Loveless Relationship

Chuck and I had what I like to call a "professional marriage" — a loveless marriage where two people are just existing together for the purpose of convenience, show, security, or as we so often hear, "to protect the children."

What makes our story different from others that we hear about, is that we were Christians at that time. Not "backsliding" Christians, but ones who really "emotionally" loved God. After the airplane scare and a similar awakening in Chuck's life, we began to teach Bible studies in our home, we went faithfully to church, and we prayed daily.

What was so sad, however, was that even though both of us were teaching others that Christ was the answer to all their problems (and in our hearts we knew and believed this to be true), in our own private lives, behind closed doors, this wasn't true at all. Our lives had become loveless and empty, just like those Israelites who entered, but never really possessed, what was rightfully theirs.

Let me back up a little and explain how we got to this point in our lives.

Coming Together

Chuck has had a beautiful relationship with the Lord since he was about ten years old. His parents were older when he was born, so a local pastor took him under his wing and discipled and nurtured him powerfully in his relationship with the Lord. Chuck's excitement about Jesus Christ continued as he entered the Naval Academy at Annapolis. Sharing the Lord with anyone who would listen, he was even asked to teach a pre-reveille Bible study, and in his senior year he wrote his term paper on Daniel's 70th Week Prophecy.

In 1956 Chuck and I were "set up" on a blind date by my best friend, Shar, who also happened to be Chuck's niece. During our childhood, she had mentioned a number of times that she wanted me to meet her uncle. Figuring he must be an old man with a cane, I replied, "No, Shar, thanks anyway."

But during our high school years when she happened to mention that her uncle was in the Naval Academy, she suddenly got my interest! So I met Shar's uncle and I married Shar's uncle, and my dearest friend became my niece!

Throughout our courtship, Chuck lovingly shared about his Jesus and all the wonderful things He had done for him. Because God's love was becoming more and more real to me through Chuck, I became aware of how much I personally needed Jesus in my own life. Although I was raised in a wonderful, loving home, I still had an emptiness in my heart that nothing seemed able to fill.

Decisions

As Chuck then shared with me and as I began to read the Bible, I realized, for the first time, that Christ had literally died for me personally. So in May of 1957 I made the biggest decision of my life: I chose to give my heart to God. I asked Him to come into my life to be my Savior. And He did.

Three months later, Chuck and I were married, and we were absolutely convinced that God had a fantastic plan for our lives together because of the wonderful spiritual foundation He had already laid.

But let me tell you that many times over the next 20 years of our marriage as I saw that beautiful vision shattered, I would go to God and ask, "What have You done, putting us together? It's a horrible mistake! We are so opposite and so mismatched!"

I hear so many Christian women today saying the same thing, and wanting out of painful marriages. I've learned, however, that God never contradicts His Word, and escape is not the answer. He wants to do a miracle in us and through us, even in the middle of our most painful circumstances.

Set Aside

Shortly after Chuck and I were married we moved to Colorado. We attended a church there, but it lacked in-depth

Bible studies, fellowship, and prayer. So without realizing it, that excellent foundation began to erode away. Over the next few years (late fifties and early sixties), in our avid pursuit of Chuck's career, our enthusiasm and love for the Lord seemed to get pre-empted by other "important things." We became too busy to go to church, to pray, to fellowship, or to read the Bible.

So for 13 years the Lord allowed us to be "shelved" and "set aside" until that airplane trip over the Rocky Mountains. How it must have grieved God's heart to see that enthusiasm, that potential, and that beautiful relationship He had begun in our hearts eroded by apathy.

About one year after the airplane incident happened in my life, Chuck happened to pick up a little book called *The Late, Great Planet Earth* by Hal Lindsey. The prophecies that Chuck had so long ago studied and taught at the Naval Academy were all right there in this book, and God used it to blow his mind! And what excited him the most was that many of those prophecies, still future in 1956 when he taught them, were now beginning to happen right before his eyes!

The knowledge that Jesus would soon return was going to change our lives drastically. God had certainly gotten the attention of both of us now!

Giving Our Lives Away

So in May of 1970, one year after the plane incident, Chuck and I and our two sons recommitted our lives to the Lord and we began fellowshiping at a wonderful, love-filled, Bible-teaching church. We made many precious friends and attended many Bible studies and prayer groups. Our enthusiasm was intense.

In those early days after our recommitment, I continually told God how excited I was to be living for Him again and how much I loved Him. I told Him He could now do whatever He needed to do in me to make me the woman of God that He desired. And, of course, I meant this prayer with all of my heart. However, I had no idea what I was really praying or how much God would require of me, in order to answer my prayer. The next five to eight years of my life would turn out to be a series of unbelievable trials and tribulations — God's "cornerings" in my life — that I was in no way prepared or ready for.

Where's the Love?

Many of the struggles we had came from conflicts between Chuck and I. I was raised by parents who gave their marriage relationship first priority. My dad was always there for my mom and her needs, as well as for us kids. I remember a very calm and undisturbed household with no internal tensions or outside pressures tearing it apart.

I didn't know any other kind of marriage existed, so it was a huge shock to find myself married to a "dynamo" who placed ten times more importance on time spent in his business and at work than time with me or the kids. Chuck worked six 18-hour days, traveled extensively (at least two weeks out of every month), and spent his time at home consumed with paperwork, phone calls, mail, business reports, and the computer.

When I complained about his long hours at the office or extensive traveling, he would just respond, "Hey, that's what you married; that's what you're stuck with!" It seemed the tighter I would grab hold of Chuck to make him change and meet my needs, the more he would pull away from me and throw himself even deeper into his business.

Chuck's job, at the time, involved taking high-tech computer companies out of bankruptcy, turning them around, making them profitable, and then starting the cycle all over again with another company. Chuck loved the wheeling and dealing of business life. He loved things like flying to Europe on Monday, being wined and dined by international companies, then taking the "red-eye special" home again on Thursday and putting in a full day at the office on Friday.

And although Chuck, with his intense drive, seemed to thrive on the challenges of his work, he was often, understandably, on edge when he was at home. He has intense highs and lows, and knowing how and when to respond to him is absolutely critical, because if you are not sensitive to this, he can be very intimidating. Chuck has an I.Q. of well over 180 and is very articulate. His verbal abilities are incredible assets in the business world, but these same attributes can be devastating if you are on the other end of an argument with him.

I used to have the best "fights" with the bathroom mirror before or after actually confronting Chuck. But when talking with him face to face, it would always come out wrong.

When Chuck would explode and hurl cutting remarks at me, I would take it all inward, and without realizing it, deep roots of bitterness and resentment began to grow and motivate much of my actions. To get even with Chuck, I'd simply become a "martyr" and for the next several days, I'd give him the cold shoulder. I wouldn't speak to him or sleep with him. Thus, our marriage became more and more strained.

It was at this point that I would go to God and ask, "Please tell me, what is the meaning of belonging to You when I am so miserable? I need Your love, but I can't find it! Where's the abundant life that I'm supposed to have when I commit to You? I've tried everything I know of, but nothing seems to work. God, what's wrong with me?"

Why Try?

Paralyzed by the emotional trauma, my behavior clearly reflected my feelings. All I could think about was my misery, my lack of love, and my crumbling marriage. As a result I let my house go to pot, I let my kids fend for themselves, and I didn't go anywhere or talk to anyone. I just stayed home, moped, and felt sorry for myself.

After attempting over and over to create a loving atmosphere for Chuck, I would finally just give up and quit trying. Why try? I felt it wasn't worth the trouble or the pretense. My efforts always seemed to end in futility anyway.

We had many other struggles that lead to our crisis. We

have never in all our years of marriage (maybe with a few exceptions at the very beginning) had an eight-to-five job with a stable income. We have either been millionaires (I think we've been there twice) or at the other end of the gamut — totally broke and paupers.

The last few years of our marriage have probably been the hardest of all, financially. We have literally lost everything. Six years ago we lost our beautiful "dream house," our cars, and our medical and life insurance through personal bankruptcy when Chuck's company failed. Then five years ago our rented home was on the epicenter of a 6.8 earthquake in California and we lost many of our own personal possessions. So, financially and materially, our marriage has been an incredible roller coaster ride.

When we were first married, Chuck used to say to me, "I can't promise you our marriage will be easy, but I do promise it won't be dull." Listen — he has kept that promise to the letter. We have been married 40 years, and believe it or not, we have moved 25 times! (You heard me, 25 times!) Our boys used to say after another move, "Shall we keep our bags packed?"

Overwhelmed with Unhappiness

Sometimes my feelings of unhappiness over Chuck's comments or our situation would consume me and just about suffocate me. They were like waves of hurt that kept breaking over me and eventually would drown me. I didn't know how to escape them; I was sick to my stomach most of the time and often depressed.

I remember at one point being so overwhelmed that I locked myself in a darkened room and cried and cried until I literally thought I would burst. But then, because I didn't know any other option, I pushed all the emotions down in my heart, locked them up tightly, forced a smile on my face, and came out to begin all over again.

I thought by burying my real emotions and putting a smile on my face, I'd eventually get rid of the anger and bitter feelings. I thought they would just go away on their own. The world functions this way, because it has no other choice. Without Jesus literally taking our hurts away, as Scripture says, "as far as the east is from the west," we are all walking time bombs ready to explode.

The truth was, when I buried my negative thoughts and emotions, I never really got rid of them at all. I only programmed them down deeper, and although I didn't realize it at the time, these buried things began to motivate much of my behavior.

Ever since I was a little girl, I've always allowed my feelings, other's responses, and my circumstances to be a barometer for my happiness and to dictate my actions. I think this is natural for most of us. If I could keep a lid on how I really felt and if I could control my circumstances and Chuck's responses, then I could give Chuck and my family whatever human love (natural love) I had. But if those buried feelings were triggered, or if Chuck said or did something hurtful, or circumstances occurred that were out of my control, then I would be miserable and not have any natural love or compassion to give to anyone. My happiness and my ability to love Chuck depended totally upon how I felt, what the circumstances were, and what he had said or done to me that day. It seemed that my whole world rose and set with how I perceived these three things.

A Phony

More than anything else at that time, I hated being a phony. To me, a phony is one who says and does something on the outside that they don't mean or feel on the inside. And that's exactly what I felt I was being forced to do.

I knew the Bible was truth. And over and over again it says in the Bible that we are to love God and, then, we are to love others. The more I tried to do this, however, the more I would feel like a failure — it just didn't seem to work. I couldn't do it without being a phoney.

Again I would go to God and ask, "Will You please tell me how I am supposed to do this genuinely? When I fake love or try to trump it up for Chuck, I feel like a hypocrite. And yet, when I don't fake it, there is no love at all to give. How am I supposed to love genuinely, as You say in the Bible?"

I found struggling to live the Christian life to be a total impossibility! How could I work up a love for someone whom I couldn't even respect anymore, let alone care for? It grieves me because I see this same frustrated and despairing state of mind in Christians everywhere today. Such deep sadness behind smiling, "plastic" faces, and I know, I know what they are feeling because I've been there!

I had no conception at that time that God's love was any different from human love. I thought God's love was poured into my heart when I first accepted Christ, and all I had to do was "name it and claim it" and His love would be right at my finger tips. I had no idea that agape love was God himself working through me. And that the only way He could flow through me was for me to yield myself to Him as an empty and cleansed vessel.

> Verily, verily, I say unto you, Except a corn of wheat fall into the ground and die, it abideth alone: but if it die, it bringeth forth much fruit (John 12:24).

God had to let me go all the way to the point of divorce before I finally surrendered and saw the things in me that were keeping His love (which was already in my heart) from penetrating my life.

Troubled Times

So things seemed to go from bad to worse, and finally came to a head the year we moved up north to the San Francisco area. Our marriage was just about over, Chuck's business had taken a turn for the worse, and we were having tremendous problems with our kids.

We had taken Chip and Mark out of their favorite high school to make the move, and they were having a tough time of it. And because Chuck and I were so embroiled in our own marital problems and so preoccupied with our own circumstances and our own hurts, we unintentionally pushed the boys out on their own to fend for themselves. Finding no answers, no consolation, and no comfort at home, they began to search for it elsewhere.

Now, so far, you might say I had a few problems: my marriage was on the rocks, my kids were getting into trouble, and we were continually moving. But you still haven't heard about the situation that God allowed in my life that almost pushed me over the edge. God must have known I was a "very hard nut to crack!"

My precious Michelle was born when I was 36 years old! She was the daughter I had prayed for and God had so lovingly given to me. Michelle, however, was born with extreme allergies and problems that evidently I had passed on to her during the last months of my pregnancy. I had basically "overdosed" on powdered milk, and developed a horrible allergic reaction which I apparently passed on to Michelle. She was born extremely allergic not only to milk and milk products, but also to the whole cow! (Milk, butter, cheese, ice cream, meat, jello, etc.)

On top of this allergy, which lasted four years, we discovered at 18 months that Michelle was hyperactive. Because the doctor believed that a chemical imbalance played a part in the hyperactivity, he advised that in addition to her milk-free diet, she be restricted from having any artificial flavorings, colorings, or preservatives. Then we discovered she was reacting to the natural silicilates in apples, oranges, grapes, etc., and I was advised to eliminate these things from her diet, also!

It was an impossible situation — trying to keep Michelle on that terrible diet while she watched the rest of us eating anything we wished. How can you explain to a two-year-old

child, "Honey, the other kids can have some, but you can't!" There's just no way you can explain it! So she would just cry harder! For Michelle's sake, I even tried putting the whole family on the diet, but Chip, Mark, and Lisa threatened to run away from home and Chuck said he would never come home!

As if this wasn't enough, at the age of two Michelle developed a mysterious limp, and began to drag a leg. Doctors at Stanford Orthopedic Hospital diagnosed it as a deterioration of the bone marrow and told us that if we ever wanted Michelle to walk again, we had to keep her off her feet and in bed indefinitely.

Have you ever tried to keep a hyperactive two year old in bed for any length of time? It was a constant battle of struggling and screaming and crying!

This was the most excruciating time of my life. We had again just moved and I was away from all my family and friends. I had huge marital problems, the boys hated their new school, and my Michelle was driving me crazy. I thought I would go out of my mind! I was losing control of everything I cherished.

I knew God promised in the Bible not to give us more than we can bear, but I was pretty sure I was "over the edge"! Again, I'd go to Him and ask, "What are You doing to me? I pray and things seem to get worse. It seems like you have abandoned me when I need You the most."

Chuck's business situation at this time was just about as tense and difficult for him as the home front was for me. But I was so preoccupied with me that I was totally oblivious to the fact that he had his own set of hurts and needs that weren't being met. Both of us were locked so tightly in our own worlds of tension, strife, and trauma that "on our own" we never could have, or would have, moved toward each other. At this point, we had no love, no communication, nor any respect at all for each other.

During this tense time, if you can imagine, we still had

Monday night Bible studies in our home. We kept inviting people to come and share God's love with us. But as our kids would often ask, "Why should these people want what you two have? You're no different from the people down the street who don't even know God. In fact, our neighbors are probably kinder and more loving to each other than you guys are."

Oh how that hurt, because we knew it to be true.

> This People draweth nigh unto Me with their mouth, and honoureth Me with their lips, but their heart is far from Me (Matt. 15:8).

As I saw my marriage crumbling before my eyes, in desperation I tried anything "new" that others suggested might help. I was desperate for any new ideas, new formulas, or new methods to improve what I knew was dying.

Looking for Solutions

Basically, what I wanted was a magical formula that would change Chuck. I didn't have the time, nor did I want to take the time, to wait on the Holy Spirit to personally direct and guide me. My motivations were totally self-centered. I wanted Chuck changed — not for his sake or for his best — but so that he could better meet my needs and desires.

I can even remember a Saturday afternoon when I insisted that Chuck sit down with me on the patio and read a new Christian book that had just come out on priorities. I remember thinking to myself, *This will certainly straighten him out and show him how far out of line his priorities are*. How arrogant of me to think that way. What absurdity to believe that "I," with my little book, could change Chuck on the inside. That's God's job.

I've come to learn that real and lasting change comes about only in God's timing and in God's way, not in my own. It's an inside-out change that we seek, a permanent change — not a temporary, outside change. "God's ways are not our ways" and we can't simply take someone else's personal advice

from God and apply it to our lives. We each need to seek the mind of Christ and His specific will from His Word for our own individual situation. Of course, this takes time, discipline, and commitment and, at this particular point in my life, it was just easier to read a book.

One of the most common ways we all try to have our needs met and our marriages saved is through the "way of emotions." As women, we often try this way first. Instead of stopping, thinking, and responding, we automatically react and become carried away by the tide of emotion. Often we end up deeper in the pits than when we began because we say and do things we can never take back.

Here's an example: Often Chuck would call from the office around 7 p.m., after I had already prepared a nice dinner, and say, "I'm sorry, Honey, but I have to work late tonight. I'll probably be home around 10 or 11."

Immediately, buried feelings of rejection and bitterness (that I had never dealt with) would be triggered and my composure would fall apart. Rather than act lovingly, as I desired to do, my voice would automatically become as cold as ice. Even on the phone, Chuck could sense my attitude change. After banging the phone down on him, anger, frustration, and hurt would totally consume me. All night long, rather than catch those negative thoughts and emotions, I would continually think about what Chuck had done. This produced the horribly tense atmosphere that my poor Chuck came home to later on that night. Looking back, it's a wonder that he even bothered to come home at all.

> Every wise woman buildeth her house, but the foolish plucketh it down with her [own] hands (Prov. 14:1).

And I was doing this brick by brick.

"Controlling" My Feelings

When circumstances between Chuck and me were calm and I was able to somewhat control and hide my true feelings, things would go pretty smoothly for awhile. But when another shattering incident would occur, my buried feelings and emotions would explode and once again direct all my reactions.

In retrospect, controlling my emotions meant covering them up so tightly and burying them so deeply that I couldn't feel them any longer. When I did this, however, I also built a huge wall around my heart so that nothing at all — bad or good — could penetrate. I not only prevented and "walled off" God's love from coming forth through me to others, I also prevented God from manifesting His love to me personally.

One of the other ways I tried to restore our failing marriage was the way of submission. There was no doubt in my mind that submission was God's will for me.

> Wives, submit unto your own husbands, as unto the Lord. For the husband is head of the wife, even as Christ is head of the church: and he is the savior of the body. Therefore as the church is subject unto Christ, so let the wives be to their own husbands in every thing. Husbands, love your wives, even as Christ also loved the church, and gave himself for it (Eph. 5:22-25).

Now this works beautifully in a family where everyone is committed to following God's plan of authority. However, when one or more of the members of the family are out of their place in that chain, or one member is not even a believer, then it has to be a totally supernatural act in order to genuinely submit at all.

So, on the outside, with a big plastic smile pasted on my face, I would obey and submit to Chuck. On the inside, however, I bitterly resented the whole thing — not only Chuck, but I also resented God, for making me have to go along with this charade!

In my mind, Chuck was the one "out of the chain of command." He wasn't loving me, so why should I have to submit to him? I felt as if I was being used and stepped on, just like a "doormat."

I understand now why I hated the way of submission so much. If we are submitting out of our own natural strength and ability and not God's, then we will feel used and stepped on, just like a doormat. If, however, we can learn to set ourselves aside and begin to operate on God's supernatural love and power through us, then it will not be us doing the submitting or loving, but God acting through us. At that point, we'll feel more like "powerhouses," certainly not doormats.

But I didn't know this back then. So, again I'd cry out to God, "Is this what it means to love one another? How can I love and submit to a man who I don't even like anymore?" Talk about hypocrisy!

Take Any Class

One of the final ways I tried to save our marriage was to find any class on marriage or relationships — anything on how to "be a desirable wife," how to "be a sexy mistress," how to "be a beautiful mother," how to "be an interesting partner," or how to learn to this or that. . . .

I'd sign up, go, sit in the front row, and take thousands of notes. Then I'd go home and immediately try to put into practice all I had learned. Unfortunately, it was still just "me" doing the work, and not God through me, so eventually it would all fall flat again.

In one of my classes, a friend had a great suggestion. "Nancy, get rid of all your kids for one evening and fix a fancy candlelight dinner. Then meet Chuck at the front door wrapped in nothing but Saran Wrap. Lure him into the dining room and then seduce him under the table.

She had a great imagination and it would have been

wonderful fun, if my heart had been in it, and if our dining room table didn't have a pedestal right in the center.

Most of the implementing I tried, however, was tough, hard work. And it's no wonder, because again "I" was the one trying to perform the work, and not God through me. I was striving to do the Holy Spirit's job. So eventually, like all the other ways, it would fall flat.

Just for a moment in those marriage classes, I would see my true self as they would share God's Word. But when I came home and encountered Chuck, I would forget what I had seen, and once again, try in my own power and strength to do what I thought I had heard. Thus, my love gestures to Chuck were not authentic, love-motivated actions prompted by God's Holy Spirit, but simply self-centered things I was doing to see if I couldn't get Chuck to fall back in love with me, and meet my own desperate needs.

The truth is, if we're not motivated by God from a pure and open heart, then there is no earthly way it will be God's unconditional love flowing through us like 1 Corinthians 13. Only as we give ourselves totally over to God, as pure and open vessels, can He then love like 1 Corinthians 13 through us.

The only thing that God needs from us is the willingness to allow Him to use our lives as open conduits to love others through. From start to finish, God must be the one doing the work, and not us!

Why Should I Be the First to Change?

However, again I was unaware of this. So finally, just like all the other solutions, I would get tired of performing and give up, especially because I never saw Chuck trying. Why should I be the first to change?

I hear this question all the time now, "Why can't my spouse change first! It's not fair!" Well, by worldly standards, it might not be fair. But as Christians we don't go by worldly standards. And the reason God says we must be the first to change is simply that our life depends upon it! Our life depends upon our own willingness to allow God to change us and to conform us into His image.

So it really doesn't matter who is the first to change, because God desires us all to change and be transformed into His image. The faster we allow God to do this, the happier we will be.

So the real problem then was with me, not with Chuck. The problem was in my holding on to and burying hurts, resentments, bitterness, anger, criticalness, unforgiveness, judgmentalness, etc. (justified or not), and not recognizing that these things separated me from God and His love. God can't fill dirty, self-centered cups and that's exactly what I had become.

Therefore, nothing in the world at that time — books, classes, emotions, submission, etc. — could have saved my marriage until I learned how to yield myself moment by moment to God (love Him) and totally relinquish myself to Him. Then and only then, His life from my heart could begin to come forth and manifest the "real love" that would eventually save our marriage.

Explosion Point

Our lives seemed to crescendo up to an inevitable explosion point and we began to talk of separation and divorce. Neither one of us saw any other way out of the pain but to escape and run. Totally consumed by my own hurt and bitterness, I arranged for a flight for me and the kids back to my folks in Los Angeles, the only place I had to go.

Two nights before the trip, however, Chuck and I got into another one of our horrible arguments. He hated these discussions because we always ended up deeper in the pits than when we began, but I wanted one more chance to get through to him, so I entered into the discussion aggressively. In response to something Chuck said, I arrogantly replied, "But don't you ever want to hear what God wants to say to you?" I meant that if Chuck would just listen to God, God would show him how messed up his priorities were.

How presumptuous of me to act as God's little Holy Spirit nagger. God doesn't function that way. So I fully deserved Chuck's response and it's one I will never forget.

Chuck simply turned to me and said, "Won't you let Him?" (In other words, "If you, Nancy, would get out of the way, maybe I could hear God.") Those four little words are burned into my memory forever.

I was absolutely shocked. I had always felt that "I" was the one who was "spiritual." After all, I was the one continually in Bible studies and prayer groups. I was the one reading God's Word and standing on His promises. And I was the one who had all my friends praying for Chuck. What on earth did Chuck mean that I was in the way of his hearing God? I sat back — absolutely stunned!

God used those four little words to blow my ears wide open. He wanted me to see what was going on in my own life: the pride, self-centeredness, unforgiveness, and bitterness that had covered over and quenched God's love in my own heart.

> Why beholdest thou the mote that is in thy
> brother's eye, but considereth not the beam that is in
> thine own eye? Thou hypocrite, first cast the beam out
> of thine own eye, and then shalt thou see clearly to
> cast out the mote of thy brother's eye (Matt. 7:3–5).

My eyes had always been focused directly on Chuck and the "speck in his eye" and I had completely missed "the plank in my own eye." As I sat there absolutely stunned, Chuck must have sensed an opportunity to tell me how he felt about us and our marriage and what he really desired in a wife. He had seldom shared his deep feelings or hurts, but this night God enabled him to share his heart as he never had before, and God opened my ears to finally hear.

He began by telling me what he had always desired in a wife. "Someone," he said, "who is easy, warm, and comfortable

51

to be with. Where I can just be myself, and not on guard or defensive. Where the atmosphere is one of love and acceptance, not one of tension and judgment.

"Someone I can turn to for constant companionship and support, a teammate with the same goals and purposes. Someone who would love me just for myself, not for what she wanted to make me into."

It was interesting that he never mentioned the things that I would have thought to be important to him: a romantic and sexy lover, a stimulating and intelligent partner, a good mother and homemaker. I think, had I been graded on these, I might have fared better.

A Supportive Partner

Every time I think back on that night in 1975, my mind flashes back to Genesis 2:18: "It is not good that man should be alone; I will make an help meet for him."

Deny it if we will, but a "help suitable for completing our husbands" is why women were created in the first place. We were created not only to fellowship with God, but to unite alongside of our men and, in love, accomplish God's objectives and His will here on earth. I don't believe we women will ever truly be fulfilled until we learn to comply and fit into the mold we were made for in the first place.

The irony was that, as Chuck was pouring out these heart-piercing truths that night, he was describing the wife I had always wanted to be but knew in my heart I wasn't. I hated the person that I had become. The acid of bitterness does horrible things to our countenance and there is a sourness, a hardness, and a harshness to the appearance of one who is consumed with anger, bitterness, and unforgiveness.

As God began to reveal all the things in my own heart that were separating me from Him (the self-pity, the spiritual pride, the hautiness, the self-righteousness), I began to cry uncontrollably. I had never seen my self-centeredness before in its true light. I asked God to forgive me for hurting Chuck so much. I had never seen it from Chuck's perspective before and I felt overwhelmed with remorse and sorrow. I confessed to God that I had held on to all those negative emotions and that, even though I didn't realize it at the time, it was sin and had separated me from Him.

A New Way to Love

That night, even in the midst of all my emotions gushing forth, I was aware of the presence of God. He kept saying to me over and over again, "Nancy, I love you. I am going to show you a new way to love — a more excellent way to love. Are you willing to trust Me?"

In my mind I responded to Him, "But God, I've tried all the ways there are. None of them have worked. There are no other ways."

Again, His response was, "I love you; will you just trust Me and choose My way?"

Finally, crying out in my heart, I said, "Okay, God. I don't want to follow my own self-centered ways anymore. I'm willing to do anything you want me to do to change. I do trust You. I do love You. Please show me Your way of love."

Then, for the first time in 20 years, I asked the Lord to change me into the woman Chuck needed instead of asking Him to change Chuck into what I needed. "Change me, Lord, into the woman Chuck just described — she is really who I want to be."

So that night I gave God all the things He had shown me that had separated me from Him — all the hurt, bitterness, and unforgiveness. I gave God all I had to give, which was me! And you know what? That's all I am responsible for! I am not responsible for Chuck and what he chooses to do. I'm only responsible for me and what I choose to do!

Finally, I had yielded my will and my life to God. Finally, I had kept my part of the bargain that I made with God in that airplane incident some six years previously. Finally, I gave Him an empty and cleansed vessel, that He could now fill.

God impressed on my heart that night that this was not going to be just a one-time choice, but that I would have to continually, moment by moment, choose to follow His way of love and not my own self-centered way of thinking. Wouldn't it be great if we could only choose once and we'd be on our (His) way. Even if we could just choose once a day — like getting dressed in the morning — and we would be able to stay in that direction all day. But it doesn't work that way. To stay in God's way, all day, is a moment by moment process. However, I must say, the moment by moment choices do get easier the longer we walk with Jesus because we quickly find out there is no other choice to make.

It had taken me 19 years from the time I first asked Jesus into my life to finally come to the end of myself, to die to what I wanted, to die to what I thought, and to die to what I felt. In other words, it had taken me 19 years to learn "to love God." Again, I had never equated loving God with John 12:24–25. But this Scripture is exactly what it means!

I had given my heart to Jesus 19 years before and I was definitely "born again." God had been in my heart all along, but I was the one preventing Him from coming forth and manifesting His life and love through me, because I insisted on holding on to my own "justified" thoughts and feelings. These negative things then acted like a wall or a barrier over my heart, and prevented God's real love from coming forth. All of these things became sin because I kept them, pondered them, entertained them, and mulled them over rather than immediately giving them over to God.

Yes, I'm Willing

God began to teach me then how, moment by moment, to yield and give over to Him all my thoughts, emotions, and desires that were contrary to His. He showed me that I didn't have to feel willing to do this, I simply had to be willing. And over the years, I have found that this is my only responsibility: to stay a willing and cleansed vessel. God has all the love I need,

He has all the wisdom I need, and He has all the power and ability I need. I simply must be willing to allow Him to perform these things in and through me.

As I began to "take every thought captive," recognize my hurts, my anger, etc., confess them as sin, repent of them, and give them over to God, God's unconditional love in my heart began to permeate my being for Chuck. And my life began to change dramatically, from the inside out. I began to experience not only a new love for Chuck that I had never encountered before, but also new wisdom to know how and when to love him, and a new power and ability to live God's way that I never possessed before. God truly had begun to teach me a "more excellent way" to live.

A More Excellent Way

Remember the example I gave earlier about Chuck coming home late for dinner? Well, about a year after I began walking in God's way of love, a similar situation occurred. Chuck called one evening around six and said, "Hey, Honey, I have a free night and I'll be home by seven. Why don't you call the boys and invite them over for dinner and we'll have a great evening together."

I was so excited, I put a leg of lamb in the oven, called the boys at their apartments, and told them to come over. Seven o'clock came and went, then 7:30, 8:00, 8:30, and 9:00. About 9:30, Chuck walked in the door — genuinely sorry, but he had gotten tied up with some very important businessmen and they had all gone to dinner together.

Now my "natural" emotional reaction was still the same as it had always been before. I have learned that "self-life" does not improve with age — it's just as ugly today as it was the first day we believed. Maturity in Christ is simply the ability to recognize that "self-life" and give it over to God.

By the world's standards, I would certainly have been "justified" to be angry and upset. My roast was burnt to a crisp, the boys and I had wasted a whole evening just waiting around, and the girls had finally given up and gone to bed. My natural reaction was to tell Chuck off.

But God had begun to show me a better way to love and to respond (a more excellent way). All night long as I was waiting for Chuck, instead of letting the "justified" anger and frustration consume me, I kept choosing as best as I could to give these things to God so I could stay an open and cleansed vessel for his love. I didn't simply bury my real feelings like I used to, or pretend they weren't there. I just kept recognizing them as they came up and verbally handing them over to God.

Let me tell you, it's hard work, constantly choosing not to go by your own feelings and emotions. But how excited and thrilled I was when, at 9:30 p.m., it was God's genuine, supernatural, and unconditional love that met Chuck at the door and not my own normal, self-centered reactions.

I genuinely felt no bitterness, anger, or frustration over what had happened because God had literally taken them all away. Chuck and I were then able to sit down and talk freely and openly about what he had done.

There definitely is a time to confront and tell the other person how you are feeling, but only when we are cleansed vessels ourselves. Otherwise, we end up deeper in the pits than when we started. When we are cleansed vessels, then the confrontation is done in God's love. We are not only freed from our own presumptions and expectations, but the one we are loving is freed to respond from his heart and not his defenses.

Chuck was so sweet, so apologetic, and so remorseful. And I know he saw the "new" responses in me and felt the peaceful atmosphere. We played games with the boys until midnight and we all had a great time.

The most thrilling part of all was that I didn't have to be a hypocrite and trump up something I really didn't feel. God's supernatural love came from my heart and it was genuine.

This genuineness and freedom is where, I believe, God

wants us all to live continually — where our hurts, frustrations, fears, and doubts are set before God, and we are willing to sacrifice what we want, what we think, and what we feel in order for His purposes and His plans to be accomplished through us.

My Diary

Many more incidents like this last example began to happen, so I decided to keep a diary. Here are a few of my favorite entries:

August 1976 — (Three months after we had the blowup and God began to work so mightily in my life): "Chuck called today while away on a business trip and said, 'Honey, the only thing wrong with our new marriage relationship is that it's no fun to travel anymore!' "

How many times I had pleaded, cried, and begged Chuck not to travel so much. But nothing ever made a difference until "I changed" and allowed God's love to become a part of my life.

September 1976 — "Chuck has begun to come home from the office at noontime now, because he says he misses my company and wants to talk."

Chuck is a total workaholic. He would never take time off for anything. Also, he has always had a difficult time sharing his personal feelings until "I changed" and God's love became a part of our relationship.

This last entry is the most precious of all. . . .

December 1976 — "Chuck asked me today, if I were single again, would I marry him? He just wanted to make sure I was happy with what I had!"

The climax of 15 years of living God's way of love happened only a few years ago. We had gone to the Great Barrier Reef in Northern Australia for our anniversary. While on that trip, in a moment of quietness and intimacy, Chuck held me in his arms and read Proverbs 31 out loud. At each appropriate verse he called me his "Proverbs 31 lady." It had been over 30 years since he had called me that.

The love that God has returned to our marriage and our family is incredible. When I stay that open channel for God's love and I keep my eyes squarely focused on Jesus to meet my needs for love, meaning, and purpose, then I am able to quit strangleholding Chuck to meet my needs. I am also able to quit trying to conform him into "my desired image" for a husband, and simply accept Chuck as he is and genuinely love the "whole package." The minute, however, I stop looking to the Lord and stop being that open channel for Him, it never fails — I grab hold of Chuck and, once again, we both sink.

The Difference

Before, I was frantically striving to live the Christian life on my own power and ability, my own understanding of the situation, and out of my own self-centered human love. I was fabricating emotions and feelings that didn't exist and burying negative feelings and thoughts that did. My eyes were always focused on Chuck, the situation, and on my own all-consuming hurts; never on God, where they should have been from the start. Not only was I a prisoner of my own negative thoughts and emotions, but I had put Chuck in bondage as well because of my own expectations and presumptions. It was an impossible situation and a vicious circle from which neither of us could have escaped without God's intervention.

Now, however, as I seek, moment by moment, to be that open vessel, I am experiencing God's genuine, supernatural love coming forth from my life. It's consistent, real, and lasting, and something I believe many Christians never see or grasp at all. I really believe with all my heart that there is no trial too big, nor any difficulty too hard that God's agape love cannot be the full remedy. But, first we must be willing.

A girl from one of my classes once said to me, "I am not willing to go God's way. What will make me willing?"

I asked her, "Are you happy? Are you content? Are you fulfilled? Do you feel loved where you are?"

She screamed back at me, "Are you kidding? Of course not!"

"Then," I said, "that — the pain — is what will make you willing!"

It's those hard, tough, perplexing, confusing, and painful corners that God so lovingly puts us in, that force us to be willing to be willing.

Truly, God has wounded me in the last 20 years, but in so doing He has healed me and given me His abundant life.

Why should we be the first to change? Because it's the only way to know His love, His peace, and His joy. These things do not come from the absence of trials, but only with the presence of Jesus.

I pray our story encourages and gives hope to anyone who sees us, that if God can return His love to us, then He can do the same for them!

God's Love never fails (Cor. 13:8).

Nancy's essay includes excerpts from her book, *Why Should I Be the First to Change?* All of her books are available through Koinonia House, P.O. Box D, Coeur d'Alene, ID 83816, 1-800-KHOUSE1.

Bonnie Thomas

In addition to speaking at women's conferences and teaching Bible studies, Bonnie also teaches on the faculty of Ravencrest Bible School and Conference Center in Estes Park, Colorado, where her husband is the director. Through Ravencrest she directs and coordinates special studies, including a bi-annual conference entitled "Reflections in the Rockies." Bonnie is the daughter of Cliff Barrows, who has been the music and program director for Billy Graham's crusades for over 50 years. Her father-in-law, Major Ian Thomas, founded the Torchbearers of the Capernwray Missionary Fellowship, headquartered in England, of which Ravencrest is an outgrowth.

Chapter 3

I told God that if I was a sinner, He would have to show me. That is a very dangerous prayer to pray. He's been showing me the truth about myself ever since.

Early in the morning on July 15, 1982, our little town of Estes Park, Colorado, was beginning to wake up. People were already lining up at the donut shop, and shopkeepers were out watering their geraniums under a cloudless blue sky. I was at home making French toast for my three boys when I stopped to answer a knock at the door. It was one of my neighbors who announced with a sense of urgency, "Bonnie, a flood is going to hit town in 30 minutes."

Standing under a sunlit morning sky, it was hard to take in what he was saying. But he went on to explain. "A young man was out collecting trash this morning in Rocky Mountain National Park, and at about 6:30 he suddenly heard a deafening noise. He looked up and saw trees flying through the air like toothpicks. Long Lake Dam has collapsed, and there is a huge wall of water headed toward Estes Park."

The town was quickly evacuated. Since we live on a mountain overlooking Estes Park, we knew we weren't in any danger, but helicopters flying overhead and radio coverage warned of imminent catastrophe. At 9 o'clock, almost on the dot, an eight-foot wall of water came crashing right through the middle of town, taking out everything in every shop and building on the main street. And with the surging river came remains of houses, cars, mobile homes, and other worldly possessions, all swept away by the force of the water.

Estes Park was devastated. Walking through town that night, we were numb. Everything was covered with mud and silt, and shop owners sifted through the debris in a state of shock. We watched as building inspectors went from building to building, indicating with a large X those buildings that were condemned. Everything seemed lost.

Today, if you ask the people of Estes Park about the flood of 1982, they will tell you that, looking back, it was the best thing that ever happened to our town.

Estes Park was one of the older towns in Colorado. Unlike the beautifully forged ski resorts of Aspen, Breckenridge, and others, Estes Park was not keeping up with the times. It was a little helter-skelter town with many cheap tourist shops and uninteresting storefronts. Individual profit and loss were the primary concerns. There was little sense of "community" effort and few people paid any attention to the streets, the cracked and uneven sidewalks, or the gaping potholes. It was every man for himself.

But after the flood came, things changed. Everyone had to start over and the whole town had to be rebuilt. People started getting together and working on a master plan to make the town beautiful. Now, in addition to the shops, there are new wide streets and beautiful brick sidewalks, with benches, trees, and flowers everywhere. Today, Estes Park, Colorado, looks like a "little Switzerland."

The reason I love the story of the flood is because it is so relevant to my own life. I once had a storefront, too. There was a great gap between the private Bonnie and the public Bonnie. And as I look back at the floods that God has brought into my life, I have to say, "Lord, it was the best thing that ever happened." Sometimes we think the floods in our lives make us what we are, but that isn't the case. The floods *reveal* what we are. In my life, there was so much that needed to be cleared out, so much that needed to be changed, and so much that was built on a faulty foundation. God has used the floods in my life to clear those things away.

Playing to the Crowd

One of the first things God had to rebuild in my life was my *sense of self-worth*. If *anyone* should have had a good sense of self-worth, it should have been me. With parents who loved me deeply and provided constant affection and affirmation, it should have come easily. But there was a problem.

From my earliest childhood, my whole life was focused on self, and on how I came across to others. Since my dad was the music and program director for Billy Graham's crusades, we used to live and travel in those circles. And I learned at a very young age how to perform. I found that you got a lot more attention by being good than by being bad — more love, more affirmation, more pats on the back, more goodies — a candy-coated life. So I learned to play to the crowd. I never rebelled, I never bucked the system. The only problem was that I wasn't being good for God's sake, I was being good for Bonnie's sake. It was pride and self-centeredness at the heart, even the heart of a little girl.

I have often compared my life to the story of the prodigal son and his older brother. According to my husband, Chris, most people in the world are one of these two people. The prodigals are people who sowed their wild oats, or maybe just wanted to. They're not worried about breaking the rules or keeping the status quo.

But I was the older brother. The older brother was caught up in his own "goodness," which looked noble on the outside. But inside, in his private life, he was immersed in anger, aloofness, jealousy, legalism, self-pity, self-centeredness, and joylessness. What fascinates me is that the prodigal son ended up in a pigsty because he was so obsessed with how *bad* he had become. But the older brother was in an internal attitudinal pigsty of his own because he was so obsessed with how *good* he thought he was. Neither one knew joy.

I was obsessed with being good, even better than that — perfect! When I was eight years old, I learned Romans 3:23 in vacation Bible school, "For all have sinned and come short of the glory of God." Sitting in my room later that day, I remember looking up at the ceiling and saying, "God, I memorized this verse today that we have all sinned, but, Lord Jesus, I really believe that I am the exception to the rule." And I wasn't being funny, I really meant it. I couldn't remember ever having sinned. That is the attitude of an "older brother."

I told God that if I was a sinner, He would have to show me. That is a very dangerous prayer to pray. He's been showing me the truth about myself ever since.

There is a saying that, at 20, all you worry about is what people think about you. At 40, you're *not* worried about what anybody thinks of you. And at 60, you realize they weren't thinking about you at all.

In those early years, I thought everyone was watching me and I could not, would not, let them down. My self-worth was wrapped up completely in becoming the best in everything. But being perfect is a heavy load to carry.

The problem with being a perfectionist is that it's all up to you. You have to constantly prove yourself to others. I always had to have feedback. If I took a dish to the potluck dinner and nobody asked me for the recipe, I felt I was a failure. If I wore an outfit and no one admired it, I would hesitate to wear it again. It was always an obsession with self.

One Christmas, my very wise husband helped me take a long, painful look at what I was doing. Not too long after Chris and I were married, our whole family came home to celebrate Christmas together. We all brought presents, and I was thrilled that everyone really seemed to like the gifts I had chosen. Then everyone started opening the gifts that my sister-in-law Nancy had brought.

For months, Nancy had painstakingly worked on cross-stitch plaques for each one of us, inscribed with our names, a verse, and the meaning of our names. And she had made *14* of them! They were absolutely gorgeous, and all day long no one could talk about anything else.

When we went to bed that night, I didn't even fully understand it, but I was depressed. And I was quiet. When Chris asked me what was wrong, I said, "Oh, nothing."

He said, "I know what's wrong with you. You are jealous."

"Jealous?" I responded. "Jealous of what? Who?"

"You are jealous of Nancy," he said. "Bonnie, you have got to let somebody else be first sometimes."

We had only been married six months. I felt like leaving him right there. You can be honest in your marriage, but that is being *too* honest.

The life of a perfectionist is a very lonely one, and it's destined for failure. Because no one can be the best in every situation, there is always jealousy, and competitiveness, and criticalness. And when failure comes (and it will), it leads to guilt, and guilt, if not dealt with, leads to depression. It's a very hard way to live.

What's wonderful to me is that in the story of the prodigal son, the father "came out" to the older brother. We all know the wonderful picture of the father running out to welcome and embrace the prodigal when he returned home. But what I love is the father coming out to the older brother — the cranky old self-centered, perfectionist, older brother who was feeling very sorry for himself. And the father says, "My son, you were always with me, and everything I have is yours."

So many times in my life, God has said to me, "Bonnie, you have always been mine ever since you were a little girl. My child, all that I have is yours, but you haven't entered into the joy of it. You have been trying to deserve it. You have been trying to earn it. You have been trying to prove yourself to Me,

and Bonnie, you don't need to! You are My child. I love you just because you are mine. Your self-worth isn't found in what you do, it's in who you are in Me."

Just as in the story of that older brother who tried so hard to do everything right, my Father has come out to me many times in the midst of my "trying," my exhaustion, and my failure. He has told me I don't have what it takes to be perfect, no matter how hard I might try. He is the only perfect One, and my life is designed to revolve around Him.

He has told me that I can't find my self-image within myself, because I wasn't made in the image of *self*. I was made in the image of God. I must go to Him to understand who I am. To search anywhere else is futile.

And He has told me that the truest thing about my life is what He says about me, not what other people say. That is such a hard thing to learn! It doesn't matter who likes me and who doesn't. It doesn't matter what people think. All that matters is what God says about me, and He says I am worth the price of His Son.

I know now that there is an immeasurable difference between trying to be perfect, and trusting the perfect One. One is bondage and the other is freedom. We must stop trying and start trusting. He will make us what He wants us to be.

Less Than Competent

As God re-directed my own sense of self-worth, He also had to deal with my understanding of *competence*. I had always been convinced that I was more than competent to handle whatever my situation in life might be. I kept mental files when I was growing up, and I had a file for everything — marriage, missions, parenting, etc. One by one, God began to pull those files out and say, "Okay, Bonnie. Think you can do it?" And I was always ready.

The first file He pulled out was missions. And I thought, *Oh yes, I'm going to go to the mission field and I'm going to turn the Philippines upside down!* I had a very sincere zeal. But God showed me I didn't have what it takes to be a missionary. I needed to be teachable, and I needed a new understanding of the power of God in my life.

I remember taking a psychological test when I joined Campus Crusade for Christ, and I knew they only called people in for test interviews if they felt like there was a problem. Much to my dismay, they called me in.

The staff psychologist said my test scores indicated that I carried an inordinate sense of responsibility for everything and everyone. He was quite concerned because, in reality, I couldn't control the responses of others. If people rejected me, I would be crushed and guilt-ridden, and in the long term I wouldn't be able to handle it. He was right.

A few years later, God pulled out another file — marriage. And I told Him, "Oh, Lord, I have been waiting for 28 years to be a wife. I can and will be the very *best* wife. I have gone to all the seminars, I have read all the books; I can do this!"

C. S. Lewis says you get married expecting heaven and what do you get? You get earth.

When Chris came into my life, it seemed to be a marriage made in heaven. But he was English and I was American. I thrived on physical and emotional closeness and affection, he was more stoic and reserved. I was not like his mother, and he was not like my father. We were raised so differently, and we expressed our love in totally different "languages."

Early in our marriage, God used another couple to help ease me through those differences. Immediately after our honeymoon, Chris and I moved to Milwaukee, Wisconsin, where he had been called to serve at Elmbrook Church. The senior pastor there was Stuart Briscoe, who had been like a big brother to my husband at Capernwray Bible School in England.

When we arrived, the Briscoes invited us to live with them until we could find a house, so we moved into their den. Looking back, I realize those four months were just what I

needed. Since the Briscoes are also from England, I was the only non-Britisher in the house, and God used that time to teach me some of the differences between American and British family life. And I learned not to take myself or those cultural differences too seriously. We laughed a lot — or they laughed at me, I'm not sure which!

One of the first hardships God had to deal with in my marriage started when Chris began to travel. During those times, I found myself experiencing terrible times of darkness and depression. I asked the Lord why I was having such a struggle, and one day while I was taking a long walk in the mountains he gave me my answer.

When I was a little girl, my father had to travel extensively, and he was often gone for long periods of time. I missed him but I had never verbalized it. That day in the mountains God spoke so gently, *Bonnie, when you were a little girl you felt your daddy never really belonged to you, he belonged to the world. Now you're feeling the same way about your husband.*

It made sense — but what was I to do with these feelings? God's answer was straightforward. Just as many years earlier, I had come to know God as my Father, now He was telling me that I also needed to know Him as my husband, my "heart's husband."

In my futile efforts to try and make my husband, Chris, the answer to my deepest longing (an impossible task for any man), he underscored once again what the Lord was teaching me. I remember very vividly a comment Chris once made to me, "Bonnie, I can't be God for you. I'll be there for you as much as I can, but you need to learn to turn to the Lord and walk with Christ yourself."

Those first years were difficult for both of us. Once, early in our marriage, we were attending a Valentine's banquet. They were giving different awards for who had been married the longest, and who had been married the shortest. Chris simply volunteered, "Well, we have been married the hardest."

He was right, primarily because I was demanding of my husband that which only God could give.

There is within every one of us a cosmic loneliness that no man in the world can fill, only Jesus. I believe Chris and I have a wonderful marriage today, but it is not because two halves make a whole. It's because two wholes make a marriage. And we are both whole in Jesus Christ.

Once God finished with my marriage file, and showed me that I am never competent apart from Him, then He pulled out my parenting file. I knew I was going to be a good mom. I had read books, I had watched other people's children, and I knew that my children weren't going to be like some of them!! No snotty noses or crabby kids in the grocery line for me! Our children would be different!

Then God gave me three boys. Three! My mother sent me a little plaque that said, "A boy is noise with dirt on it." How true!

I thought I knew all the answers, but I didn't have the answers for *my* children. My boys didn't fit the mold in the books or in my files.

I remember once when Chris went to India and was gone for five weeks. My children were one, three, and four. I thought I was going to die without his help on the home front. About the third week, it seemed all hell broke loose.

I remember walking into my living room and shouting at God, "I am fed up; I can't take it anymore. I am so tired!"

And I heard His still small voice inside me saying, "I'm not. I never grow tired or weary."

"God, I don't understand boys! They say the ugliest, crudest things. I just don't understand them!"

And I heard God say, "But I do. I have all the wisdom in the world to raise boys."

"But God, I don't have any more strength. I don't want to go on. I want to quit. I want to walk out."

He said, "Well, I can work in you to *will* as well as to do

— you can do all things through Me. I'll strengthen you."

I spent 15 minutes telling God everything I wasn't, and He spent 15 minutes telling me everything He was. And when we were finished, I heard the Lord Jesus say to me, "Bonnie, you and I share the same body and if one of us is okay, we can go on . . . and I'm feeling fine!"

That changed everything for me. I realized, in the words of a favorite song, the key to being a Christian is "not in trying, but in trusting. It's not in running, but in resting. It's not in wondering, but in praying, that we find the strength of the Lord."

Once again, as a parent, He showed me my own incompetence. But not only that, He showed me himself. My father-in-law, Major Ian Thomas, once gave me a quote that has proven to be an anchor in my life. He said, "I can't, and God never said I could. He can, and He always said He would."

With this foundation, we have worked to make a home for our sons, a refuge where they can be real. It's a place where they can be who they truly are and not who we think they ought to be. Of course, by God's grace, we are guiding them and training them in the ways of the Lord. But I know that, ultimately, God himself is the one who will have to take hold of their lives in His time and His way. Home is a place where they can fail, be loved, and be discipled, but most importantly, where we can talk it all out, rather than "stuff it," "perform it" without real understanding.

Not too long ago, my oldest son graduated from high school, and it was one of those moments in life that is a milestone. After 18 years of giving and giving and giving, I began to sense that something was coming back. Now, once in a while, he'll put his arm around me and call me "Momsy" as he loves to do, and he'll ask me how I'm doing. And all of a sudden, I feel like I'm getting something more here than just a son or a child, I'm getting a friend. It's as if the love has come full circle.

Bonnie Thomas

A Friend of God

In the most recent years of my life, this concept of "friendship" has taken me to a new place in my relationship with God.

The journey started on January 19, 1995. I was scheduled to meet with my committee in planning our bi-annual conference, Reflections in the Rockies, and I was supposed to give them a vision for what God wanted us to do.

But I was exhausted. I had just been through the final chapter in my mother's four-year battle with cancer. She had died on December 8, and following her funeral I had returned home to a house full of company for Christmas. On top of that, Chris was again in India for five weeks. It seemed to take everything I had just to make it through the day, much less to come up with a vision for the future.

As I got into the shower that morning, I remember praying, "God, I've got to know what to tell these women. I'm supposed to motivate them. Would you please give me something, and please hurry, because You only have these few minutes in the shower to do it!"

Suddenly an old hymn came to mind that I hadn't heard in years, "*O master, let me walk with Thee, in lowly paths of service free, Tell me Thy secret, help me bear the strain of toil, the fret of care.*" And standing in the shower, I said, "Yes, Lord, please walk with me."

But a little whisper in my heart said, "That's not what the song says." I recalled in my mind the lyrics, and sure enough, the words were "O master, let ME walk with THEE." And I thought, *Oh, that is different, isn't it?*

As I thought about it, I remembered a recent Sunday school lesson about Abraham and how "Abraham believed God and it was credited to him as righteousness and he was called God's friend."

Then it hit me. He was called *God's friend.* I have always called God my friend, but it never occurred to me that possibly

I could be His friend. I knew I needed God to walk with me, but it had never crossed my mind that maybe, once in a while, He would like me to walk with Him. At that point, I realized that knowing the friendship of God is Christianity 101. Becoming a *friend of God* is perhaps Christianity 401. I wanted to understand more.

About that same time, some friends at Ravencrest Bible School, knowing what I had been through, arranged to take our kids so that I could get away for a weekend to rest. I decided to go down to an abbey in Boulder where our staff often goes for their retreats. It's a wonderful, quiet place. That's where I began my Bible study on the friends of God.

The first person I came to was Abraham. James 2 tells us that Abraham was a friend of God, and it says that he, Noah, and Enoch walked with God. Not that God walked with them, but they walked with God.

Abraham trusted God so completely that when he was asked to do the seemingly impossible in sacrificing his son, he didn't question or complain. He simply did what God told him to do. Wasn't it beyond reason to think that a man of 100 years could father a child? Wasn't it beyond reason for Abraham to walk up that mountain and sacrifice the son whom God had promised would be the future of the whole Jewish nation? Wasn't it beyond reason to think that God would somehow do something He had never done before, that He would bring the dead back to life?

Yet Abraham so trusted the heart of God that even as he was ready to bring down the knife and kill his son, he believed that God would raise Isaac from the dead. What a trust!

I heard God say to me that weekend as I studied the life of Abraham, "Bonnie, will you be My friend and trust Me in the dark? Will you trust Me when life and everything around you is beyond reason?"

Having lost my mother, there were so many things I didn't understand. I didn't understand why it had to be so horribly cruel and painful at the end. I didn't understand how my father could re-marry so very soon after Mom's death. And I didn't understand the struggles in my relationship with my mother. I had wrestled with it for years.

But again, I heard God saying to me that weekend, "Will you be My friend and just trust Me when you don't understand? Will you just believe that I am with you in life, in death, in darkness, in light?"

When Chris and I were first married and living in Milwaukee, he was the singles pastor at Elmbrook Church. We became close friends with a number of people who had been married and were now "single again." I began to notice that some of the same cracks in their marriages were becoming evident in my own marriage. The more time I spent with them, the more concerned I became: Would our own marriage fall apart?

I will never forget the night I shared my anxiety with my husband. Vehemently, he rose up in bed, took me by the shoulders, literally shaking me, and said, "Bonnie Thomas, I will never divorce you. Will you not believe me? I love you and you are hurting me because you will not trust me."

His words spoke to me so deeply. If we, being evil, can give such a loyal, committed love, how much more can our Father in heaven who loves us so dearly?

That is a God I can trust. I told Him that weekend, "Thank You, Lord. We're going to go on together. And I know that when I cannot trace Your hand, I can trust Your heart."

The second person I found in the Bible who was a friend of God was Moses. Exodus 33 talks about Moses going out to the tent of meeting in the wilderness, and the presence of the Lord coming to talk with him. The Bible says the Lord spoke to Moses "as a friend speaks with a friend."

In the still silence of those abbey walls, I felt like God was asking me, "If you are My friend, will you listen to Me? Will you be quiet and let *Me* talk sometimes?"

I know that it is one thing to study God's Word, but it's something else to listen, to hear His inner voice speaking deep within your soul. That kind of conversation makes for an intimate relationship.

One morning about that same time, I woke up around 4:30 or 5:00 in the morning. I was suddenly wide awake, and I felt like God was telling me to get up and spend time with Him. Mind you, it was not in an audible voice, but like a whisper in my heart.

I walked into the living room and picked up my personal copy of Oswald Chambers' *My Utmost for His Highest.* I turned to January 12, and the title was "Have You Ever Been Alone With God?" The message hit home like an arrow, but at the bottom of the page was a footnote in my husband's handwriting. I have no idea why it was there in my copy of Oswald's book, but for some reason he had written, "Loneliness is God knocking at the door."

It just jumped off the page at me. I was still grieving for my mother, and with Chris gone for five weeks, I was in deep loneliness. And I was still wrestling with the difficulties I had experienced in my relationship with my mother.

In response to God's "knocking," I opened my Bible to Hebrews where I had been reading earlier. Early that morning, the Lord gave me a revelation about my mother and me that was so freeing! In just that one moment, when I let Him have time to speak, and I had time to listen, He gave me the answer to the problem that had plagued me for years. I learned in that day that a true friend of His is someone who takes the time to listen to Him.

As I continued my study that weekend in the abbey, I came to another friend of God. His name was John the Baptist.

John had a powerful ministry of preaching and "preparing the way" for the Lord. His whole ministry was built around pointing to the One who would come. When Jesus did come, people soon started turning away from John and following after Jesus. When that happened, John's closest friends came to him, saying "Rabbi, that man who was with you on the other side of the Jordan, the One you testified about, He's baptizing now and everyone is going to Him."

Reading between the lines of what they were saying, John explained to them that he was not the Bridegroom, but the *friend* of the Bridegroom. He said of his Lord, "He must increase, I must decrease."

This is a wonderful picture of the heart of John who did not come to point to himself, or to build his own kingdom, but to point only to the Bridegroom.

That's when I felt God asking me, "Will you be My friend and point only to Me, not to yourself? Because if everyone thinks you're wonderful and yet they don't see Me in you, you have failed miserably in the purpose for which you were put on this earth."

I've had to learn that God wants me to be a steppingstone in people's lives, not a monument stone. Like John, we're not to be hurt when people move on with the Lord and leave us. He is the one who is to be everything to everyone!

During the weeks leading up to my wedding, our family was privileged to have Corrie Ten Boom stay with us in our home. I was being given a bridal shower, and my mother asked Corrie if she would give the devotional. I was thrilled, but at the same time, knowing she had never been married, I wondered just what she would have to say.

She began, "Bonnie, my verse for you is, 'May Christ be formed in you.' " Then she told a story about how, after the war, she and her brother Willem used to run refugee camps for children who had lost their parents in World War II. They would have two or three hundred kids in camp at a time, and they would take care of them, play games with them, and teach them about the Lord Jesus. The bonds were strong.

One day Willem had a great idea. He wanted to take a picture of all the kids. So he took them out to the playground and lined them all up in squiggly lines. He hurried up to the roof to take the picture, but instead, came down and started moving the children around.

"Can you move a little to the left? Can you get behind her? How about coming forward? There — that's right!"

He kept giving instructions, and the children started complaining, "We want to go play. The sun's too hot. How long will this take?"

Finally, when Willem got everyone positioned just right, he went to the roof and took the picture. The film was developed, and several days later, the excited children gathered around to see the results. When they looked at the picture, they were totally surprised to see that right across the playground, they had spelled out the word "J-E-S-U-S."

I'll never forget what Corrie said to me then. She told me, "Bonnie, in your life, God is going to move you. Sometimes He's going to say 'Bonnie, fall back behind Chris . . . now move a little forward . . a little to the left . . . a little to the right.' "

She continued, "I've never been married, but I believe that what God wants to do as you make yourself available to Him day by day, is to write the name 'J-E-S-U-S' across your marriage. That's my prayer for you and Chris."

There are times when I don't like it, when I want to run away, when I'd rather be playing. But that's when God says to me again, "Will you be My friend and point to Me, not yourself? Will you let people see Me written across your life?"

I am convinced that true maturity in Christ involves becoming a friend of God, and I learned a great deal during my time alone at the abbey. But I know, too, that this life is just a time of engagement, a time of promise. The wedding is still to come.

After my mother died, my dad re-married and decided to sell the family home in South Carolina. It was a beautiful place, and I remember going there for the last time with my sister. At one point she turned to me and said, "This home has been the most wonderful place in all the world. If we love this home, how glorious will be the home He is preparing for us? I can't even imagine it!"

It is so true! And if today I love the Lord Jesus as my friend and Bridegroom, what will the marriage be like? The best is yet to be!

Rexella
Van Impe

Along with her husband, Dr. Jack Van Impe, Rexella is the highly respected co-host of the weekly global news telecast, "Jack Van Impe Presents." As an active board member of Jack Van Impe Ministries International and co-producer of the television program, Rexella is also jointly responsible for the production of the ministry's teaching and evangelistic video cassettes. She reports international news each week and has interviewed hundreds of influential world leaders as well as recognized Christian writers and scholars. An accomplished musician and author and a celebrated conference speaker, Rexella was given the prestigious "Outstanding Woman in Ministry" award by the International Women in Leadership.

Chapter 4

If I could give my life a title, it would be "A Very Different Life," because it has not been ordinary. It's been unusual, exciting, blessed — anything but ordinary.

"You know, I'd give anything to marry a successful minister the way you did," a well-meaning, Christian woman once said to me.

Her statement made me smile because when I married Jack, he was hardly what the world would call "successful."

I met Jack during my second year of college. A struggling, young evangelist who was already out of school, he was a close friend of my brother. Jack often visited with our family, and we all adored him. As my affection for him grew, it didn't take me long to realize he had many of the qualities I wanted in a husband.

Although I was only 19, and several years younger than Jack, we decided to get married.

"I will have to ask my parents," I told Jack when he proposed.

As a Southern girl born in Missouri's Ozarks, I had always honored my parents' wishes for my life. Besides, I knew that my father, a typical Southern gentleman, respected Jack. I also knew that Jack had long ago won my mother's heart. Still, I wanted and needed their approval — which they willingly gave along with their blessing.

Little did I know at the time the wonderful joys — and heartaches — that awaited Jack and me in the years ahead. Over the years, the Lord taught me many important — and difficult — lessons: unquestioning submission to God's will, total reliance upon Jesus, complete trust in God, and submission to my husband.

Many people tell me I inherited my mother's gentle spirit, but they don't know the lessons I had to learn to become the kind of wife the Lord wanted me to be.

When we were first married, Jack and I lived on the love offerings we received from our evangelistic meetings. Having come from a home that had been quite secure, I quickly had to adjust to the unpredictable state of "living by faith." I'll never forget our first evangelistic tour of California, which lasted eight weeks. We came home with $80 dollars after all our expenses were paid.

Many months we wondered if we would have enough to pay our bills, but God never failed us. Although we did without many things, I never coveted more than what God provided for us. The desire for an elaborate home or a secure future never consumed me. I only wanted, truly, what God desired for us — and I knew that would be enough.

How did a 19-year-old bride develop such yieldedness to the Lord's will? I believe God had been preparing me for a life of full-time ministry many years before I met Jack Van Impe.

"What Is Wrong With Me?"

My first lesson in the importance of unquestioning submission to God's will came when I was a teenager. My two brothers and I were raised in a large evangelical church of about 1,700 people. The church — and music — were a big part of my life from the very beginning. My parents were very supportive when it came to developing their children's talents, so I started singing when I was five years old, and I was playing the piano at ten.

The pastor — and the church as a whole — were committed to helping young people follow Christ and serve Him. Out of about100 teens in our youth group, probably 15 later went into full-time missions. During my high school years, I committed myself to living a Christian life and even led some of my friends to the Lord.

One day when I was almost 17 I told the Lord, "I will do anything for You except go to the mission field." I knew the hardships this could entail.

I felt living among the natives in some foreign jungle was beneath me. A sudden case of appendicitis, however, changed my perspective. As I was lying in the hospital bed and dealing with complications from the surgery, the Lord gently came to me each day. He would say, "You know, Rexella, you really are not that submissive. I may call you to go to the mission field."

"Lord, I told You I'd do anything but go to the mission field," I replied.

During those long hours in the hospital as I read my Bible and prayed, the Holy Spirit began to move in my heart. Under deep conviction, I broke down and said, "God, what is wrong with me? I will go to the mission field; I don't care if You bury me there. I want to be wherever You want me to be."

That day I surrendered my will to God, and He lifted the burden. The Lord didn't want me to be a foreign missionary; He wanted my will.

At the same time, the Holy Spirit began to reveal an even deeper and more serious spiritual problem in my life: I was not truly born again.

Although I knew all about the Lord, had led other people to Him, and was a leader in my youth group, I was as lost as any tribesman in the most remote part of the earth. As an active member of our church, I was singing in the choir, performing solos, and participating in a girls' trio — but in my heart, I knew something was missing.

One night after singing a solo for the evening service, I went to the back of the auditorium and sat down. The Holy Spirit convicted me and, as I left the church in tears, my dad saw me out of the corner of his eye. He followed me out to the car where I was sitting and crying. "What is wrong with you, Rexella?" he asked.

"Daddy, I don't think I'm saved," I replied, brushing aside the tears.

I will always be thankful to God for my father's reply. He didn't try to talk me into it; he didn't say, "Rexella, you'll embarrass me and the whole family if you admit you're not born again. You've been baptized already; what is wrong with you?"

He just looked at me and said, "Be sure."

That night I went home and meditated on the things God had been showing me about my life.

A few nights later, while I was in my bedroom weeping, my older brother came in. Four years older than I, Bob had always been a great example to me. He had known since he was ten years old that God was calling him to preach.

"I don't think I'm saved," I admitted.

That night, there beside my bed, my brother led me to Christ.

"Be Sure"

For a long time I had deceived myself. Knowledge and works seemed to take the place of true faith in Jesus Christ. I knew all about Him, but the verse, "That I may know Him in the power of His resurrection and the fellowship of His suffering" (Phil. 3:10), was not real to me.

I knew all about Jesus just as I knew all about the president of the United States, but I didn't personally know Him as Lord of my life. I had deceived my family, the church — and even my own heart.

It's so easy, today, in our society to deceive ourselves about our spiritual condition. That's why, I think, so many young people fall away. They have been raised in the church and know all about the Lord, but they have never been saved. As a result, their hearts become callused to the gospel and often are the hardest to reach.

Many people in our churches today struggle with the same misgivings and doubts that I had. My experience has enabled me to lead others to Christ, including pastors' wives, who wonder, *Am I truly saved?* Many have gone to Bible school, married ministers, served in their churches, and yet they have never surrendered their heart to the Lord.

My husband, Jack — who was reared in night clubs — realized before the age of 13 that he was lost. He knew that he needed the Lord.

As for myself, I was like the Pharisees whom Jesus addressed in the Bible. Despite all my good works and seeming piety, I never had peace until I had Christ. There were always doubts.

From the moment I truly repented, asking Jesus into my life and my heart — from that moment until now — I've had the utmost peace and assurance of my salvation. Outwardly, I didn't change much, but on the inside the sins of the spirit began to melt away.

In fact, those of us who don't give in to the sins of the flesh must be doubly careful about the sins of the spirit. Those of us who think we are "righteous" because of our good works fail to see our desperate need for God's forgiveness. Once we realize the condition of our heart and confess our sin, however, we experience so much repentance, joy, and peace that we never doubt our salvation.

My advice to others is the word my father gave to me: "Be sure."

I Got the Message

As newlyweds, Jack and I were constantly on the road for all but about 12 weeks out of the year.

When Jack wasn't preaching or ministering to people, he

spent time memorizing, studying, and developing a repertoire of messages. In addition, he practiced his accordion several hours each day. Jack has been called "the walking Bible" because he has memorized over 14,000 verses by subject — the equivalent of more than the New Testament.

While Jack was studying and memorizing, I spent long hours alone in hotel rooms. This was difficult since, like most women, I enjoy talking and sharing experiences and problems with my friends and family.

Since I had no close loved ones with me, I learned in those early days of our traveling ministry to share my desires and feelings with Jesus. On the road, I spent my days and nights talking to the Lord.

During those long hours of being alone, I became a student of the Bible. As I leaned on the Lord, I found that all of my burdens and questions were addressed in the Bible. God's Word began to sink into my life, and I began to grow not only in years but in wisdom.

Before long I realized that spiritual maturity was critical to our ministry. During our evangelistic meetings, Jack would preach and then invite people to come to the prayer rooms. As a young woman I had to counsel people with complex problems like promiscuity, homosexuality, and drugs — situations that many Christians seldom encounter. When confronted with a new situation, I turned to the Bible, knowing God's Word could meet every need.

The challenge of being an evangelist's wife taught me to dig into the Word to find answers for the difficulties people were facing in their lives. As I searched the Scriptures for others, I also found answers for myself.

One day I asked God, "How can I experience more joy and contentment?" The answer came when I studied Galatians, Ephesians, and 1 Peter, where God's Word speaks to Christians about the husband-wife relationship.

God impressed on me that I would be happier, find true

contentment, and have everything I desired, if I would learn to be the kind of wife God wanted me to be. I knew I needed help in this area.

In the early part of our marriage, if Jack would say something like, "We're taking this crusade to St. Louis," I would immediately say to myself, *This is the wrong time.*

The Holy Spirit, however, would stop me and say, "God is guiding Jack. Get behind him with all your heart. Back him up 100 percent."

Remember the trip to California when we came back with only $80 above our expenses? After that seemingly fruitless tour, I had been tempted to say, "I told you so."

The Holy Spirit, however, closed my mouth and said, "If you question Jack's will, you question My will — because it was My will that you go to California."

In my heart, I knew why we had made that trip. Many people had come to Christ during that tour — which was the reason for going to California in the first place. After all, I had married an evangelist!

Later, I realized that the trip had been a tremendous success. As the years went by, I saw that our "$80 tour" had brought us into contact with many brothers and sisters in Christ who would later open doors for us — doors leading to the expansion of our ministry and our ability to reach far more people.

I had been tempted to be impatient, but God saw the whole picture. And Jack — because he had so diligently sought the will of God — knew that the Lord had a higher purpose in mind.

"Be still, and know that I am God," the Holy Spirit spoke gently, humbling me and teaching me once again the value of submission.

I was finally starting to get the message!

True Fulfillment

Today, I am thankful I learned the true meaning of submission early in my marriage. It hasn't always been easy, but as I struggled to be faithful to the Lord, He has been faithful to me.

God tells husbands, "Love your wives as Christ loved the church and gave himself for it, enough to die for them."

God knows that women will respond to that kind of love and devotion. As a result, submission to a husband who truly has your best interests at heart can be pure joy.

With so much of God's Word in him, Jack couldn't help but become a wonderful husband. The more Jack grew in his relationship with the Lord, the easier it was for me to respond and be the kind of wife God wanted me to be.

As I learned simultaneously to submit to God's will and to my husband's will, Jack and I began to work together more closely as a team. When God laid something on Jack's heart, I tried to back him up and fully support him.

In today's society — against the backdrop of feminism and the women's liberation movement — it is difficult to help wives understand that to be liberated, they need to do it God's way. Submission is the secret to true freedom — not only in our relationship with Christ but also in marriage.

I often have the privilege of meeting and rubbing elbows with women at the executive level both in the television industry and in the corporate world. Although many of them have reached the top of their profession, often their lives are void of true joy and fulfillment.

Emptiness seems to be the sign of our times. Why? Because without a purpose in life, we have no reason for living. Many people today are searching for the meaning of life, but they are looking in the wrong places. They avoid all constraints and think that "submission" is a dirty word.

I am thankful that God has given me opportunities to share with these successful women that the direction they are going leads to a dead end. I am able to point them to the written, living Word of God as the answer to their emptiness and loneliness. After all, it was a lesson I had to learn myself.

Rexella Van Impe

$4 Million in Debt

Not too long into our ministry, we had our first city-wide crusade. From there, the Lord began to open many doors for us across the country.

We were quite a team. Jack became the flaming evangelist, while I sang, played the piano, and spoke at our ladies' luncheons. We were two hearts blended together for God, eager to see souls saved and lives changed. Our greatest joy came after the meetings when Jack and I would counsel with people and lead them to the Lord.

As our ministry grew, we realized that the way to reach the lost in this modern age was through television. We began developing ideas for a program. Since Jack and I worked so well together as a team, we envisioned a format similar to the one we use today. Jack's ability to draw on the Bible makes it possible for me to ask any question God lays on my heart because I know Jack will have the answer.

I believe God showed us the direction we should have gone, but we listened instead to consultants who were advising us. They suggested we use an entirely different format in which I interviewed people, and then Jack gave a message. Since we were never together on the screen, the format lacked personality and warmth. It may as well have been two separate shows.

Next, these consultants recommended we give away, on the air, the products being produced by our ministry. We wanted to do that, but we also knew that air time and production costs are very expensive.

Once again, we set aside our good judgment and listened to the consultants. Within a short period of time, over a million people responded to our free offer! After honoring our promise to give away all the products, we suddenly found ourselves $4 million in debt.

Our television program was just getting started, and already our debts equaled the amount we had budgeted for the entire year of ministry. How could we keep going and pay our bills?

Some people in our situation might have said, "We'll just declare bankruptcy!" In fact, we knew other ministries who had done just that. They simply told their suppliers of books and Bibles, "Sorry. We can't pay you."

Jack refused to do that. Instead, we went to our knees and asked God's forgiveness for ignoring His will. Then Jack called every one of the creditors and said, "You'll get your money. Be patient." I believe that God rewards integrity.

We took the program off the air for a couple of years, and eventually paid off our debts. Then we reorganized our program format the way Jack and I knew God had originally designed. We started again, and from there our ministry doubled, quadrupled, and grew into an international television outreach seen by millions of people.

Bitter or Better?

That experience taught me some very valuable lessons. First of all, I learned the meaning of true trust. In the beginning of this crisis, I cried out to God, "Why is this happening? We believed we were doing what You wanted us to do. How will we survive?"

Whenever I questioned the circumstances, the Lord answered me from His Word: "Trust in the Lord with all your heart, and lean not upon your own understanding. In all thy ways acknowledge him, and he will direct your paths" (Prov. 3:5–6). Those words became a reality as we trusted that God was guiding us. We clung to the Lord and to each other.

I also learned the meaning of humility. It's embarrassing to say, "We're practically bankrupt." Out of many tears, I found peace in being humbled as I learned to rely on God's promise to restore our finances and our ministry.

It was easy for us to identify with Job in the Bible who learned deeper faith and trust in the Lord through his disastrous losses and public humiliation. Like Job, I'm sure we had friends at the time who probably wondered, "Boy, what in the world is wrong with them? Why is God permitting this in their lives?"

I have learned never to judge a brother for his mistakes or condemn those who experience devastating setbacks. Our crisis taught me to pray for those who are going through trials and tests — that God will not only bring them through, but bring them through better. Trials will make you either bitter, or they will make you better.

Although Jack struggled for a while in his own spirit to know which way to go and what to do, he came out stronger and better for the Lord. And once we crossed to the other side, Jack knew exactly which direction to take.

When we finished paying off all of our debt and were finally out from under that heavy burden, Jack told me, "We're going to build a new international headquarters!"

Before I could catch my breath, Jack continued laying out God's plan for our ministry. "We're going to build our own television studio, and we're going back on TV — all within one year."

Our bookkeeper came to us and said, "Dr. Van Impe, are you sure you want to do this? You just got out of debt."

Jack simply replied, "I know."

Within weeks we went from wondering, *Why did this happen to us and our ministry?* to a very definite course of action. Jack knew exactly what God wanted for us.

It was marvelous to come out of that crisis — like Job's experience — into a brighter, better situation than we could ever have imagined.

Within that first year we had paid for the headquarters building. In addition, our television network was growing and we had our own studio. I can't help but smile when I see what God has done. We are so thankful, and praise the Lord for His faithfulness. Even more wonderful is the fact that this is only the beginning. We are praying that our ministry will continue to go forward.

Reaching the Unchurched

Jack Van Impe Presents now airs on over 800 stations and is seen each weekend by millions of people throughout the United States, Canada, all of western Europe, in the Caribbean, and in South Africa. We also now have a radio network that reaches the Third World with the same program by radio.

We are told that our telecast is probably viewed by more unchurched people than any other religious telecast. Why is that? Because we deal so much with current events.

When people read in the newspaper about earthquakes, wars, and the New World Order, they wonder, *What is going on?* Then they hear Jack and me discuss the biblical relevance of events taking place around the globe, and they realize that God is in control.

People in the entertainment business and in government watch the program regularly to get God's perspective on the news. In fact, in our capital of Lansing, Michigan, we're told that the first topic of discussion for the state Senate on Monday morning is what they learned on our program on Sunday night. Jack's adeptness at taking international events and correlating them with the Bible makes our program unique. In fact, I believe God wants to use our ministry on an international basis to reach the lost around the world.

Many other television programs are reaching Christian viewers and doing a marvelous job. But I'm so grateful that God has given us the privilege of penetrating into the world of those who are unsaved and unchurched.

Throughout the world, church attendance has dropped dramatically. In England, Norway, Sweden, and Denmark less than 5 percent of the people go to church regularly. With the decline in church attendance has also come a longing for spiritual truth. We are thrilled to have the privilege of helping provide the answer to a searching world.

Recently, a TV station in Los Angeles added *Jack Van Impe Presents* to their programming, and 180,000 people watched us on the first viewing. In New York City a record was broken as 500,000 viewed the program over a Labor Day weekend in just that one city. It is clear: people are desperate for answers.

Often someone will say to us, "You are our church."

We want to meet our viewers' spiritual needs, but the goal of our ministry is to present the truth of the gospel through prophetic events happening in our world today. When people do accept the Lord through our program, we encourage them to find a Christ-centered, Bible-believing, local church.

As we continue to reach more and more people, Jack and I feel so blessed that God has chosen us to do this work. At the same time, we feel a great responsibility to present the truth — no matter what the cost.

While we were off the air for awhile and working through our financial difficulties, Jack published a very controversial book.

The Lord had been speaking to Jack's heart about the need to unify the body of Christ. In this book, Jack stated that denominational differences over secondary issues should not divide us. It took a lot of courage for Jack to take this stand.

Jack wrote that anyone who truly believes and receives Jesus as their Savior belongs to the body of Christ. Other issues, Jack said, are distinctive as far as your denomination and the way you choose to worship, but they are not distinctive as far as your faith. All believers who lift up the Lord Jesus and preach the born-again experience are one body in the Lord.

After this book was published, many seaparatist Christians felt they could no longer help support our ministry. As a result, we lost a great deal of our sponsorship and suffered financially for a couple of years.

Once again, God rewarded Jack's obedience and integrity by expanding our base of support. Even more wonderful has been the way people of all denominations sense our love for them. Whenever someone asks, "What denomination are you?" we reply, "We like to be called Christians."

Our answer usually illicits a smile and a nod of agreement from most people. They understand that love, faith, and unity are more important than denominational barriers.

"I Will Never Ask Again"

My life has been filled with some very exciting and blessed experiences involving our ministry, but I've also had my share of personal hurts. I'm grateful for the trials because I know God has used them in my life and in the lives of others. One of the greatest struggles in my life centered around my desire to have children.

Since we had been blessed with a very full life and a wonderful marriage, Jack always felt fulfilled. Like most women, however, I longed to have children. In fact, my dream was to be blessed with a large family.

After struggling with health problems and undergoing surgery twice in order to improve the possibility of conceiving, I couldn't understand the reason I was not allowed to have a baby. In the depths of my heart, I identified with Hannah's weeping for a child. It hurts to be a childless woman when you have the heart of a mother. I cried out to God, "Lord, is it because I wouldn't be a good mother?"

Then I tried bargaining and making promises: "God, I'll keep on serving You; I'll keep traveling with Jack. I'll take the children with me."

Then one day, I got terribly sick. While in the hospital, the doctors told me that I would need a hysterectomy. I refused the operation, convinced that God would answer my prayers and permit me to conceive despite my medical condition.

During this time, Jack prayed with me, supported me, and encouraged me. But my husband could not deliver me from the source of my frustration because God was teaching me another lesson.

One day I was praying all alone and just as clearly as could be, the Holy Spirit spoke to me and said, "All right, you will have your request, Rexella. I will give you a family, but it will not be my directive will for your life, it will be my permissive will."

And with that, I bowed my head and said, "God, I'm sorry. I have been beating on the gates of heaven for all these years. I don't want my will; I want Your will. More than what I desire, I want what You want for me."

Finally, I said, "I will never ask again."

As soon as I surrendered to God's will, He delivered me from self-pity. I knew He had other blessings planned for me. With renewed vision, I was able to focus on doing the work He had given me to do.

Not long afterwards, I had a badly needed hysterectomy. "Why did you wait so long?" the doctor asked after the procedure. I realized that my stubbornness had almost cost me my life.

Peace came! No children, but contentment. Then, I realized I was not childless. God had given me spiritual children — thousands of spiritual children.

Just a few weeks ago, the director of our television program came to me and said, "I just want to thank you for being my spiritual mother."

Time and time again, in different ways, the Lord allows my mother's heart to be filled.

Recently a little ten-year-old child wrote to me. "Dear Rexella, My daddy, my sister, and I watch you and your husband every week. My mommy just died, and my sister needs to have her tonsils out. But she won't do it until you tell her that she should. So would you please take a picture of your throat, if you ever had your tonsils out, so that my sister will do it?"

I didn't send a picture of my throat, but I did mail this family a video about heaven and told them, "This is where your mommy is."

In my note to the little boy, I said, "You are doing a wonderful thing, taking care of your sister just like my big brother did for me. Tell your sister that I had my tonsils out at just about her age. She's going to be all right. Tell her not to be afraid. I'll be praying that her guardian angel will be right there with her."

That little boy truly blessed this "mother's heart!"

Today, women still come to me in tears and confide that their bitterness and pain over childlessness is hurting their relationship with their husbands and with the Lord. Now I can take them in my arms and cry with them because I understand how they feel.

Then I tell them, "Having children is a tremendous blessing, but knowing and experiencing God's love is the greatest gift of all. If you accept that and fill your life with His will — His purpose for your life — then you can know satisfaction and fulfillment."

I can say that with all sincerity because the Lord has done that for me. How I praise Him for his goodness and faithfulness!

"God Loves You"

Through our ministry, I have been blessed to meet, counsel, and witness to thousands of people of all ages. Along with Jack, I have had the privilege of leading many of them to Christ.

Jack had never felt that we had an empty nest. He always believed that God had given us thousands and thousands of spiritual children. I rejoice that these dear ones are the family on whom God wanted me to shower my love and focus my attention. In fact, God has given me the desire of my heart — a large family. How do I know? Because we receive 70 — sometimes 100 — pounds of mail each day.

"Does it frustrate you that you cannot be present with all your viewers when they receive the Lord?" someone once asked me.

"You know, it does at times," I replied, "but I have to remind myself that someone far more important than Jack or Rexella Van Impe is there with them. When they repeat that prayer, the Holy Spirit is present."

How do I know? Because Jesus says, "No man can come to me, except the Father which hath sent me draw him."

When a viewer asks Christ into his life, in that moment, he is born again by the Holy Spirit. I can rest assured, knowing He will guide them, comfort and help them.

Jesus said, "If I be lifted up, I will draw all men unto me."

That's all Jack and I do — we lift up Jesus — and it is He, along with the presence of the Holy Spirit, who guides new Christians into all truth.

When people write to us, we send our viewer's information, which tells them how to grow in the Lord. Hopefully, they will find good churches and allow God to continue to work in their lives.

At the end of each program, we make the statement, "God loves you, and so do we."

A few weeks ago, a young girl wrote to me and said, "Rexella, I was going to take my life. I watched your program, and when you said that at the end, I said to myself, *God loves me, and so do they.* That was the turning point. I didn't commit suicide."

Another young woman wrote, saying she was a pastor's daughter who was raised in the church. Then she had two illegitimate babies, got hooked on cocaine, and left home. She next told us what happened while she was visiting her parents in Florida.

"My father loves your program. While visiting, I watched it with them. I want you to know that I truly prayed that prayer with Jack, and I have been born again. My life is turned

around, I am off cocaine, and I am going to be the kind of mother God wants me to be."

Jack and I have come to this important conclusion: We cannot turn this world around. The world is going to get worse and worse, according to the Word of God, and the millennium will not take place until Jesus returns.

When He does come, Jesus Christ will put an end to all the violence, destruction, and turmoil that is destroying people's lives and the world around us. He will bring peace for that 1,000 year millennium — but not until then.

Until Jesus returns, our goal is to help people realize that with everything going on around them, there is one place that they can look — and that is upward. They can look to the Lord Jesus for salvation and to His Word for guidance in their daily lives. Jack and I are merely clay in the potter's hands.

"No, It's Not Time!"

A number of years ago, an incident occurred that had a powerful impact on my life. For a long time, I could not share my experience publicly. It was so precious to me that, like Mary the mother of Jesus, I just pondered it in my heart for many years.

During a trip to Belgium, Jack and I were in a terrible car accident. The entire right side of our car was taken off, and I was thrown out into the street.

I was dying.

I distinctly remember ascending to heaven and leaving my body. As I looked back, I saw Jack praying over me, holding me, and crying. I remember saying, "I'm so sorry to leave you," but I wanted to go. Then instantaneously, I was back in my body.

This accident happened years ago — just before we were to begin our television ministry. It was as if the devil wanted to take me out of the picture. But God said, "No, it's not time." With that, I was lying on the streets of Brussels, Belgium, the car totally demolished, and Jack bruised from being knocked about.

As I lay there, a person appeared and put a blanket over me and said to Jack, "She's going to be all right." I remember hearing this voice and trying to look through the blood in my eyes to see who had spoken. But all I could see was a faint image — an outline — and then he was gone.

Jack and I truly believe that my guardian angel had appeared to comfort us. I was taken to the hospital emergency room with this blanket over me. Then, somehow, the blanket disappeared. I wanted that blanket, but it was gone.

My entire right side was mangled, and my head was the only part of my body that didn't have glass imbedded in it. I was in a cast for weeks and weeks, and it took me six months to heal. The opening week of our telecast, I was still in a partial cast. "Lord," I prayed, "I don't have the strength to do it."

He countered my doubts and replied, "I'll be your strength. I'm going to see you through this."

"But I'm not ready," I argued.

Again He answered, "Rexella, haven't you learned that you can trust Me? Your life was almost taken, and I sent you special word that you would be all right. You haven't learned to trust Me yet."

I broke down and wept.

Those six months of recuperation were a turning point in my life. God did so much for me, and I had some very special times with Him. I could write a whole message on how He ministered to me and changed my life. From that time on, I had an inner strength that empowered me to keep going.

I'm here today because God put my body back together. The only part that wasn't hurt was my face. Today, because of some wonderful medical intervention, I have virtually no repercussions from the accident.

God has done a glorious work in my life.

For many years, I could not share this experience — mainly because I couldn't talk about it without crying. Also, I wanted to be able to present what happened in a way that was pleasing to God.

The devil meant it for evil; God meant it for good. I know now that the Lord has some special things for Jack and me to do.

Secrets of a Successful Marriage

As a young bride, I remember thinking that being married to an evangelist was going to be glamorous. While it has certainly been rewarding, I must admit: evangelism is hard work. Evangelism is setting your heart to the task and not letting anything sidetrack you.

Along the way, I have had hard choices to make. Every choice I made, however, took me to a new plateau. I look back now and wonder, *What if we had done this?* or *What if we had decided that?* Our whole life would have been different.

I thank God that He has not only done a marvelous work in my husband's life, but He has also done a deep work in me as well.

Without my past, I could not be the person I am today. God put Jack and me through some very special experiences, and they have been glorious. Some have been mountaintop experiences, and some have been deep valleys. But without the valley experiences, we can't mount up with wings of eagles.

It wasn't easy to say, "I will never have a child." It wasn't easy to go through financial disaster or through the car accident. But those were special tests God had for us, and I can only say, "Thank You, Lord, for the valleys so we could exalt Jesus on the mountaintop."

What a mountaintop experience — to reach the world for Christ!

As I say these things, I do not glory in the flesh. When you've gone through the valleys, I don't think it's possible to take the blessings of God and glory in the flesh. I know that God puts us through those special circumstances in order to mold us so He can use us. While they are not always pleasant experiences, they are so necessary.

I know that the mountaintops and the valleys in my life have been much richer because of my relationship with Jack Van Impe. It is more than I can put into words. We have virtually never been apart. We have lived together, worked together, and done everything together. Ours is more than a husband-wife relationship; it's a best friend relationship.

Because Jack and I have had a good marriage, it was easier for us to go through the traumatic times. The hard times built our faith in the Lord, developed our character, and cemented our lives together. As a result, we are willing to go through whatever God brings our way.

Recently, we were having breakfast in a restaurant, and a gentleman who works with another well-known ministry stopped by our table. He said, "Let me ask you something. Give me just a quick answer as to how you've had a successful marriage."

I thought for a moment and then said, "Number one is love, number two is loyalty, and number three is laughter." These three ingredients have always stood out in our marriage and, consequently, have helped us get through the difficult times of testing.

I have great respect and admiration for Jack. He is the head of our home and the head of our ministry, yet he has always made me feel that I am one with him. He has never taken advantage of being the head. Instead, he has taken my hand and led me all the way.

Jack is called the "walking Bible" because of all the verses he has memorized. But he hasn't just memorized them; he has appropriated them into his life. Anyone can memorize the entire Bible and not be a great man of God. In Jack's life, God's Word is real and alive.

God didn't call me to the mission field after all. But He has given me a mission in life that is greater than anything I could ever have imagined or hoped for — and I praise Him with all my heart.

It has been such a joy for me to share life with a man of Jack's caliber; to share his ministry — and some day — to share his reward.

To receive information on Jack Van Impe Ministries' books and tapes, write or call:

Jack Van Impe Ministries
P.O. Box 7004
Troy, MI 48007-7004

(810) 852-2244

Barbara Barker

Barbara is the wife of Frank Barker who is the senior pastor of Briarwood Presbyterian Church, a congregation of over 4,000 located in Birmingham, Alabama. Frank was one of the original founders of the Presbyterian Church in America (PCA), a denomination organized in 1973. The PCA was formed to uphold the fundamental teachings of the Bible such as inerrancy of Scripture, the deity of Jesus Christ, and salvation by grace. In addition to serving alongside her husband, Barbara is a highly sought-after conference and seminar speaker.

Chapter 5

When Frank came home that afternoon, I met him with "I love you" rather than with "Why did you even bother coming home?" He nearly fell backwards out of the door.

It's a real thrill and a real blessing to be able to share my testimony with women across the country. It isn't a new story, I've told it before, but it's the most exciting testimony that I've ever known because it's the one that God brought into my life!

My Plans

I grew up in Birmingham, Alabama, and even from a very young age, I definitely thought *I* had a terrific plan for my life. During those years, my whole world revolved around ballet and I pursued it with all of my heart. Even at the early age of 12, I was fortunate to have had the opportunity to study in a ballet school in New York.

I believed in God, I was in a church, and it seemed as though I had my life pretty well figured out. I was convinced that my ballet career was going to be dependent on God's blessing, and God's blessing was going to be dependent on how good a person I could be. So I worked *very* hard at being good and I thought this relationship must be paying off, because every time I went for an audition, I would get the part. It looked as though I was surely going to be a "real ballerina," and it was just a matter of time.

When the time came for me to go off to college, I chose

Northwestern University in Chicago. I had a scholarship to study ballet in the city, and I immediately became involved with a group of dancers who performed in the city of Chicago. But just when my eyes were wide with expectation that the world was beginning to open up in front of me, summertime came and my daddy decided I needed to come back to Birmingham. He was afraid that my head was screwed on a little crooked up there. So reluctantly, I came back to Birmingham to dance with a summer group, feeling that this really was *not* the steppingstone in my career that I was looking for.

Nice Girls Like Me . . . Bad Boys Like Him

After being home for a couple of weeks I received a letter from a young man I had grown up with in Birmingham. He was about five years older than I, so he had graduated from high school before I got there and he was out of college before I started. But I did remember him from the time back when I was in the seventh grade and he was a senior in high school. He was the lifeguard at the pool, and I remembered sitting around on the side of the pool, listening to all the older girls talk about him. His name was Frank Barker and he had a very "bad" reputation. And I remember thinking in my moral little heart, *Nice girls like me would never go out with bad boys like him.*

But several years had passed and I was now reading this letter from "bad" Frank Barker. He was in flight training in Pensacola and was coming to Birmingham for the weekend, and for some reason I'll never know, he wrote and asked if we could go out on a date.

I always say the reason nice girls like me don't go out with bad boys like him is because they usually don't ask us. Because when I got that invitation, I was really excited about going out with him! Frank came up and we went out, and he was bad, just like I had heard. And I was fascinated. Somewhere toward the end of that evening, we were dancing. He was slightly inebriated, and he said in my ear, very romantically, "You know something, I love you and you're the girl I want to marry."

Well, I figured bad boys said things like that to dumb girls like me at times like this, so I pretended like I really didn't notice. But somehow, when I went back to dancing in rehearsals on Monday, that conversation was what I thought about all week long. I kept rehearsing the whole week and thinking about everything he had said. And I thought he couldn't really have meant it, but still it was fun that he said it.

Then I got a letter from him in the middle of that week. He said, "You know, what I said, you probably thought I said it because I had been drinking. But I want you to know I really do love you. And I really do know you're the girl I want to marry. And more than anything, I want to hear you say that you love me."

I wrote back real quickly and said that was really sweet of him and I appreciated his sentiments, but that I had a career to think about. And before I ever would stop and consider a serious relationship, I had to fulfill all of my dreams in that area first. And I would never tell anybody I loved them until I had thought about it for a long time and was very sure.

So I *did* think about it for a long time — until the next Friday. And I was very sure. It really surprised me, and everyone who knew me, but for some reason, I was really in love with that "bad" navy pilot. I decided I was ready to consider the option of being a wife instead of a ballerina.

When Frank came back to Birmingham and I told him about this great change in my heart, it scared him to death. He responded, "Well, I think you need to get out of school before we talk any more about serious plans."

Waiting . . .

So I went back to Northwestern. I'm not very gifted academically, but for the joy that was set before me, I endured the next three years of my college education along with a full program of dancing in the city. When I graduated, I flew out to the West Coast to meet Frank as he came in from a tour on a carrier out in the Pacific.

When he got off that ship he was very different. His language was all cleaned up and he didn't drink. He just seemed really kind of quiet. I figured, "Well, he's probably matured a lot from flying jets off aircraft carriers in the Pacific."

We had a wonderful week. I stayed with his commanding officer and there were all of the parties and things associated with incoming squadrons. But when it was time to go home, he had not said a word about when we were going to set any date for marriage.

Finally, as he put me on the plane, he said, "Barbara, I really need to get out of the navy before we talk about a date."

Well, if a man's not going to marry you, there's nothing a girl can do but wait. So I went to Houston, Texas, and got a job with exciting people doing exciting things and just waiting for those weekends when he could come to Houston to see me. And finally, the day came when he was going to get out of the navy, so I knew this had to be it. He came to Houston and he said, "Barbara, we're not going to get married now, either, because I'm going to seminary and be a preacher."

Well he was about the most unlikely candidate to be a preacher that I had ever seen. He was morally improved, to be sure. But he was so quiet. He didn't love old people and he didn't love children and he wasn't even religious. I thought, *Well, he's probably had some close call in the navy, and bargained, "God, if you'll get me out of this I'll do anything — I'll even be a preacher!"*

I knew he was a man of his word, and that he would go on to seminary and he would find out that he was not supposed to be a preacher and he would come home and marry me. That surely couldn't take very long. So I just left my exciting world in Houston and came back to Birmingham and started dancing with shows and doing things to pass the time until Frank realized that he had made a mistake.

After about six or seven months, he came home one weekend and he said, "Barbara, we still can't get married. I've got to get out of seminary. In fact, we're not going to get married at all."

He had gotten to seminary and realized he wasn't a Christian. And he didn't know how to become a Christian. But he had the idea that he had to get rid of anything in his life that could hinder him in his pursuit of religion, and I was his number one hindrance. So he got rid of me.

Didn't We Have a Deal, God?

And with that, my life literally fell apart. I no longer had the option of the dance career and I had no husband. And after having expended all of the 22 years of my life toward two goals, they were suddenly gone. My first response was just to shake my fists in God's face. Didn't we have a deal that if I was very good and went to church and did all those things, that God would bless me? Instead of blessing me, He had pulled the rug out from underneath me and left me with nothing.

The next thought that came to me was, *How do you know there is a God? How do you know that's not just something they tell you when you're little? They say, "If you'll be good, Santa Claus will come to see you and when you're big, if you're good, God will bless you."*

The more those thoughts began to germinate in my heart *— If there is no God, who's running this show? What is there you can be sure of in this world? —* I thought, *There's nothing you can be sure of. It's all just fate. It's just what's going to happen.*

As those thoughts festered over and over in my head, I became very disoriented and basically just panicked. I decided I didn't want to be around if there was nothing you could count on and nothing you could be sure of, especially if there wasn't anybody up there working things out.

So I decided to leave — permanently! My grandfather had always told me that when you died, you were "absorbed into the primal essence of life." So I didn't believe in heaven or hell, I just believed I would get "absorbed into the primal essence of life" and that was better than living the way I was

living. I was not brave enough to use a gun or a knife, but I thought, *I could take some pills.* I went to the medicine cabinet to find something to take. The only problem was that my family was very healthy and the only thing I could find was a giant bottle of aspirin that my daddy used for his bursitis. I took the whole bottle and lay down across my bed — to get "absorbed into the primal essence of life."

But I didn't get "absorbed" into anything. I woke up and I was very alert. I knew where I was, I knew what I had done. I knew what day it was. My mother was standing beside the bed and she said, "Barbara, wake up. What's the matter with you?" I woke up and opened my eyes. She said, "You've got red splotches all over your face."

She took me to the doctor, and without anything more than a cursory investigation, he said, "My goodness, you've got a good old adult case of the red measles." Then he sent me home to recover from the red measles in a dark room.

Where Has It All Come To?

I lay on the bed in that dark room and realized I wasn't there by accident. One afternoon, my older sister Anita came to visit me. She had been a "real" Christian from an early age but she was that legalistic kind of Christian who never wanted to have any fun and often cried because she thought I was "going to hell" because I was a ballet dancer. As far as I knew, all she did was go to Bible studies with these little old ladies and study charts. There was just nothing about her life that was very appealing to me. So, although I felt myself to be moral and "churchy," I didn't want any part of her kind of religion.

But her life had recently gone through a radical change as she had come into the freedom of knowing Jesus in a more personal way. She came into that dark room and sat down on my bed, and said, "Barbara, I have prayed for years that God would bring you to the end of all of your self-sufficiency so you would see your need of Him."

At first that offended me. I thought, *See my need of Him!*

Barbara Barker

Why, I have been among that very "artsy" crowd in Houston and Chicago and I've dated that "bad navy pilot" for four years—but I've always been to church, and I've always been morally superior to everybody around me!

But seeing though my deception, she began to explain to me what sin truly incorporated. She told me that sin was breaking God's law. It was failing to love Him with all of my heart. It was failing to love my neighbor as myself. Sin was self-righteousness. Sin was independence from God. Sin was the lack of a grateful spirit. Sin was all kinds of things that I had never before thought of as sin.

And in one afternoon, God the Holy Spirit used the Word of God and my sister to convince me that, even though I was "churchy and moral," I was one of those people the Bible spoke of as a "wicked, undone sinner," and that all my righteousness was as "filthy rags" to God. Although I had never believed in heaven or hell, as she began to show me these realities in the Bible, I acknowledged for the first time that there were indeed such places. I saw that there truly is a God to whom we all must answer. And I knew, being a "sinner," I was one of those who deserved that "just penalty for sin" — which was death!

Then she left me. Now I have said many times since then that I am grateful I didn't die that night because I would certainly have gone to hell. But on the other hand I am grateful that she did leave me, because for one night I realized my helpless, hopeless condition before a holy God. I understood that if you have already sinned and broken God's law you can't "make up" for it. I also realized that even if I had an eternity I could never pay for my sins. I wondered how a person could ever be right with God. And so for one long night I literally felt those flames of judgment.

I never fully understood how to get out of my predicament until the next morning when my sister came again to see me. I know now why they call the gospel the "good news." For truly when one fully realizes the extent of the "bad news" — the good news seems wonderfully *good*! On this visit my sister told me that although I would never live a life pleasing to God, nor be able to personally pay for my sin, that is what Jesus Christ had done for me. Jesus Christ — God the Son — who loved me so much that He was not willing to let me die, but had come to live on this earth "in mortal flesh," was subject to every temptation I would ever experience, and yet kept the law perfectly. Then He had voluntarily paid that debt of sin for me with His perfect life, which I could never do. She further explained that all I had to do was acknowledge what He had done for me, receive Him as my Savior, and trust His payment on my behalf. And then she added that I would have to "commit my life to Him."

Well, now that really sounded strange: I wanted that gift but I was terrified of the cost of totally committing to Him. What did she mean, commit my life to Him? How did I know that what He wanted and what I wanted would be the same thing? Is that just a blanket statement, "You're going to give Him your life"? I was one of those people who said, "Suppose He sends you to Africa?"

So I didn't give my heart to the Lord that night. I can't believe it — but I didn't. I sweated through hell another night. But the next morning — although I didn't know the Scripture — the truth of Romans 8:32 came home to my heart. *Barbara, if God spared not His Son for you, but delivered Him up for you, how shall He not also through Him freely give you all things? Does it not make sense that if He has already done the ultimate in sending His Son to die for you that He would not meet every lesser need in your life?*

With that thought in my heart, it seemed to me God was saying, "Barbara, for 22 years you've had your life and you've lived it and you've directed it. What has it come to? It's come to a crashing halt." I figured that if He'd chased me down to this place and loved me that much, then I could trust Him with the rest of my life.

Barbara Barker

New Life

So, I got down on my knees on the patio behind our home, and I gave my life to the Lord — lock, stock, and barrel. I got off my knees that day and although my heart in the flesh was still broken into a million pieces, I had a confidence and assurance that I had Jesus. Somehow it didn't matter where He led, it was going to be all right. I knew I could trust Him.

So I went to those Bible studies with all the little old ladies who studied their "charts." I went anywhere people were studying the Bible and anywhere people were talking about knowing Christ, or where they were praying. I'd go get right in the middle of them to hear what they would tell me about the Bible. I would go wherever people were praying and have them pray for me. It was wonderful. I had a secure little Christian nest.

But I made a big mistake. I began leaning on people to tell me what the Bible said and I was counting on other people to pray for me. I lived vicariously through other people's experiences of trusting Christ and praying. But God had saved me for something much better than that. So He picked me up out of my secure little Christian nest and moved me out to the West Coast and dumped me right in the middle of a place where I was really hurting and I was really struggling. I would go to churches and tell them I was a new Christian, and that I needed to grow, and the preachers would say, "Yes, at your stage of life everyone goes through this new stage of self-realization" or something like that. I would say, "No, I was born again." And they would look at each other like I didn't even know what I was talking about. I would be dancing and I would tell the other dancers that I was a new Christian. And they would say something like, "You know, she's from the Bible belt and everybody down South is like that." Nobody understood what I was talking about.

"I Want You to Know ME"

My circumstances got harder. There was no one to pray for me. There was no one to tell me what the Bible says. I was

111

sure that a novice like I was couldn't read the Bible and understand it. And I didn't know all the "thees," "thous," and "if thou wilts," and all the words that my praying friends had used. I didn't feel like my prayers were adequate. So I was cut off from my new-found security.

Finally, one night in absolute desperation, I fell on my knees in my apartment all by myself. I just called out to the Lord. "God, I just can't take this by myself. You've got to send me some help." And although I didn't hear voices, it was as if the Lord stood right behind me and said, "Well, come unto Me all ye that labor and are heavy laden. Take My yoke upon you and learn of Me; for I am meek and lowly in heart, and you will find rest for your souls."

It was just like the Lord was saying, "Barbara, I want you to come and know *Me*. Not through other people. I want you to *know Me*." It was a whole new revelation. It was as if I had prayed, and I had talked to God, and I knew He heard me and I knew He was answering me. I didn't know the right words — I just called out, and I knew He answered.

Then I found out He had sent me a teacher, His Holy Spirit. As I got into the Bible, I just said, "God, You've just got to show me something." And I would open the Bible and although I might find something that I didn't understand, I would also find something that seemed to have been written directly to me. I was so excited, I would go show it to everyone. And they would look at me like I was crazy. But God was talking to me! I became so hungry for the Bible's teaching that I could understand, it didn't matter about the parts I couldn't understand. Finally, I asked God to let me have a Christian friend. Almost immediately God used me to lead the model who lived upstairs to Him. We were both pretty dumb, but since there were now two of us, we had an official quorum for a Bible study. Our Bible study consisted of my reading a verse and telling her what I thought it meant and then her reading a verse and telling me what she thought it meant. Although I'm sure the church leaders would not have approved of this self-made doctrine, it was sufficient to cause us both to really learn to grow and to know the Lord.

Then we recruited a ready-made Christian, and then another, and then God even used both of us to lead somebody else to the Lord! Soon there was a whole Bible study group of us — dancers, models, all these "strange" people. We were all so ignorant, but we were coming to know something that was so real.

Finally, after about a year, I decided God must want me on the mission field. So I came back to Birmingham to apply for missions and prepare for something other than dancing. But all the Bible colleges I applied to turned me down because they didn't think I could be a Christian if I was still dancing. I was in my room one afternoon, filling out an application for Moody Bible Institute. They had at least written back to me and wanted to have a little more detail about what I did.

An Old Friend

While I was filling out that application, my mother came to the door and said, "Barbara, there's a telephone call for you." I've never understood how I knew who was on the other end of that phone . . . but I did.

I whispered, "Hello." And sure enough, it was that "bad" navy pilot who had gone to seminary to work his way to heaven. But some powerful things had happened. While he was in seminary, he had met an air force chaplain who had led him to faith in Christ. After finishing seminary, he had come back to Birmingham to start a new church in a little storefront out in an area called Cahaba Heights, which was, at the time, out in the "boonies of the boonies." He had heard that I was home and wanted to go out for coffee.

There's no way to describe what that night was like. Four years had passed but I still loved him. I had never quit loving him. Years earlier I had given him back to the Lord because that was all I *could* do. I never knew whether I would ever see

him again. And yet there we were, "going out."

We went to a little coffee shop near one of the malls and sat there for four hours. He wanted to tell me what God had been doing in his life in the last four years and I wanted to tell him four years' worth of what God had been doing in my life. Our words just seem to tumble all over each other's until 12:15 — I remember the moment. He reached across the table and took my hand, and I thought the butterflies were going to fly out of my ears. He said, "Barbara, why do you think God saved us for each other and brought us back together?"

I opened my mouth and was going to say, "I don't know, but marry me tonight before you change your mind again." But when I opened my mouth, another voice came out and this voice said, "I don't know, but until I know what God is doing, I don't want to move one step closer."

That represented a miracle of mammoth proportions. But I realized what God had done in my heart. I had come into a relationship with Him that was so precious I didn't want to jeopardize it, even to have, humanly speaking, what I wanted more than anything in the world.

Storefront Wedding

So we did wait, and we did pray, and we finally were convinced that God had indeed brought us together to be a team in the ministry. In that little storefront in Cahaba Heights where our church started, we were married. My mother almost died because we weren't married in the beautiful church where she had been married and where my sisters were married. Frank's mother almost died because we weren't married in the beautiful, newly restored chapel of their church in the front of which was a huge stained-glass window that had been dedicated to the "Glory of God" in honor of his grandfather. His grandfather's name was even printed in the colored glass. Instead, we chose the storefront where God had brought us back together to serve Him.

So on a Friday afternoon in November 1961 we were

married in what I'm sure was the most beautiful service that has ever been. No one could sit down because there wasn't room for both chairs and people. We were married by the air force chaplain who had led Frank to Christ. It was truly a storybook occasion.

Frank, suspecting retaliation from his friends who had married before he became a Christian, had made elaborate getaway plans for leaving the church after the wedding. At the given time a car came down to the parking mat outside the church to whisk us away to another car hidden in the nearby woods. As Frank hurriedly pushed me into the waiting car, my sister who had lead me to Christ hugged me and pressed a piece of paper into my hand. We then sped away form the church. (Actually no one chased us at all. Apparently his old buddies didn't know what to do with a preacher! All Frank's plans were unnecessary and he sulked for 50 miles.)

We were halfway to Montgomery before I remembered this little piece of paper that my sister had put in my hand. I always say that when you've finally got the man you've been in love with for eight years, you're not interested in more letters from your sister. But, I opened that little piece of paper and read under a light on the highway what she had written: "Seek ye first the kingdom of God and His righteousness and all these things shall be added unto you." We pulled off the highway in front of the Clara Neal Motel and asked the Lord to let that be the story of our lives, that we would seek Him first and let Him add to us as He would.

It was a wonderful, incredible beginning of our life together. But it only lasted a week.

The Preacher's Wife

We came back to Birmingham and I found out that if I had ever thought that he was an unlikely candidate to be a preacher, I was an even more unlikely candidate to be a preacher's wife. I didn't know how to cook. I didn't know how to play the piano (all preacher's wives play the piano). They didn't want me to teach Sunday school because I wasn't schooled in doctrine. The only thing I could do was dance and nobody in the church wanted me to dance for them.

We had three babies in two and a half years; I had never baby-sat, I had never changed a diaper. Frank never seemed to be home. If he was home he was on the telephone. There were always people who needed him. I felt abandoned. I felt totally inferior to everyone and inadequate for everything. There was no area in which I felt significant anymore.

I became very angry at Frank. I was very angry at these babies that kept coming. I was angry at those people in the church who were taking him away. And the worst thing of all was that I had to go around looking holy because I was the preacher's wife.

I would go to church and smile at people and say, "Oh, God bless you," and "Oh, praise the Lord," and inside, my heart was just getting eaten up with bitterness and anger. The only person I could let it out on was Frank. He would come home and walk in the door and I would start on him. I would say, "I don't know why you married me. I am utterly miserable. You're a horrible husband and a horrible father and I'd leave you if it weren't for that church of yours."

Finally, I became so miserable I couldn't read my Bible. I couldn't pray. And I lost the assurance of my salvation because I could see nothing in me that was real. Nothing in me that was truly responding to God. I became so desperate that I again felt like, "I've got to take my life and get out of here."

But the problem was that now I believed in heaven and hell. And if I wasn't a Christian, I knew where I would go, and I couldn't risk it. But on the other hand, I just couldn't stand living either.

Come Back to the Fountain

I finally began to think about those four years of closeness with God and I knew that it had been real and not psyched up. And if it was real then, it's got to be true now. So I did just what God put me in that corner to do. I fell down on my face by the sofa one afternoon. The children were 2-1/2, 1-1/2, and 6 months, and I don't even know where they were. I just said, "God, You've got to give me some help." And again, He was faithful. Although there were no words, it was so clear to me what He was saying: "Come back to Me all ye that labor and are heavy laden."

That afternoon God showed me something: "When you had nothing, Barbara, I was everything to you. And then I gave you your human heart's desire and you took your eyes off of Me and you put them on Frank. You wanted him to supply you with all that only I could give. You've gone to a broken cistern that can't hold water and you're wondering why you're dying of thirst. Come back to the fountain of Living Water and your life will be filled up again."

Another thing He showed me that afternoon was a picture of Adam and Eve in the Garden. God showed me that when He made Adam, He gave him a job to do — to cultivate a garden. Then He gave him a wife as a helper to do what He had called Adam to do, not to distract him from it. God was telling me, "Barbara, I gave you to Frank not to distract him from what I called Him to do, but to encourage him. It was not to be marriage versus the ministry. It was to be marriage *is* the ministry."

God also showed me a lot of other things that day. When Frank came home, I met him with "I love you" rather than with, "Why did you even bother coming home and I'm miserable." He nearly fell backwards out of the door. But God did something in my heart that hasn't stopped yet. He began to build our marriage.

In the meantime, God had worked in Frank's heart to show him I did have legitimate needs also and those needs were worthy of his attention. And God began to build a marriage that is the most precious thing that I could think of this side of knowing Jesus.

Secrets of a Fulfilled Woman

The World Wants to See Jesus

Since that time in our lives, Frank and I have watched together as God has done astounding things. But there was something else that God wanted me to learn in those early years that would change my life and my heart for the ministry. And to get my attention, he used Sloppy Joes.

Frank always encouraged an "open door" kind of policy in our home, and that seemed to come a little easier for him than for me. At one point, he was spending time as a liaison with a group of boys who belonged to his old high school fraternity. Since most of them didn't know the Lord personally, Frank decided to invite them over to our house so we could spend some time with them and have a chance to share Christ.

The only problem was that I had absolutely *no* money and no way to feed 30 hungry boys. But I knew enough to trust the Lord, and just at the right time when we were down to the wire, a check arrived for $25. It was great! I knew I could make Sloppy Joes for 30 boys with $25.

But when the boys started arriving, I was stunned. They all brought *dates* with them! And apparently there was so much interest in what we were doing that people just kept coming and coming through our front door.

There was nothing else to do but to just serve up the Sloppy Joes and go as far as we could. But an amazing thing happened. Even though I only had enough for 30 boys, somehow we just kept serving as more and more people came, and *we never ran out*. We found out later that 99 people had come through that line, and incredibly, there was food for everyone!

But the best part of the story for me was what God taught me through it. On that day, it was as though God showed me with perfect clarity that there is a world out there that wants to see Jesus, not Barbara. He showed me that He would be our provision in every place and we could trust Him for everything! It was a powerful turning point for me. And in all the years since, as we have made it our passion to make Him known, He has been faithful in every way to provide all that has ever been needed.

The Prayer

I remember one night back in that little storefront church shortly after Frank and I were married when I knelt with him to pray. Looking at him, I knew that he was not an eloquent, outspoken, vibrant, charismatic kind of person, and we were in a tiny storefront church out in the middle of nowhere. But he prayed, "Oh, God, make us a mighty church to reach the world for Jesus." I remember thinking, *Oh, bless his heart.*

But do you know what? I began to watch as God's plan unfolded. It's not by might, it's not by power, it's not by programs, it's by the Spirit of God. The church we serve in today represents people who believe God. They are not necessarily people with great resources or gifts, but they are people who came to a vision . . . and that vision was to know Jesus and to make Him known.

God answered the prayer that Frank put before Him that day. And I can't thank Him enough for the privilege of being a part of it and for having been allowed to witness firsthand His great faithfulness.

Briarwood has been vital not only in Birmingham, where they helped turn the city "upside-down" with the gospel of Christ, but literally throughout the world. With an annual missions budget of over $2.2 million and an unwavering commitment to their "first love," they are truly "a mighty church to reach the world for Jesus."

In addition to the hundreds of activities in which Barbara serves alongside her husband, the Lord has also entrusted her with one very specific responsibility for which He prepared her many years ago. She serves as the founder and director of the Briarwood School of Ballet, a ministry of Briarwood Church, where she oversees the training of over 400 young "future ballerinas."

Dottie McDowell

Dottie is the mother of four children and the wife of Josh McDowell, traveling author and lecturer with Campus Crusade for Christ. She assists Josh in editing his materials and works with him on special projects such as videos, international matters, and Operation Carelift, a humanitarian aid effort to the children of Russia. Together, Josh and Dottie have co-authored four children's books and are currently working on a children's Bible story book. Dottie has served on the staff of Campus Crusade for almost 30 years.

Chapter 6

The drama was right out of a movie script as I watched them move closer and closer to each other across the crowded floor. Then when they finally reached each other, I held my breath as they reached out and — shook hands! I was elated! There was hope — all was not lost!

The hardest thing I ever had to do as a new Christian was to put a letter in a mailbox. It was a letter addressed to the young man I had once planned to marry, and I knew that, once received, it would bring an end to our relationship. So I walked around and around the mailbox for an hour before I finally opened the slot and dropped the envelope inside.

Like so many other things at the time, that day marked the end of one chapter in my life and the beginning of another.

Searching

Several years earlier, I had come to Northern Illinois University as a young freshman looking for answers. And the one thing I was seeking more than anything else was the answer to the question, *Who is God?* Even though I had been loved and raised in the very best of circumstances, the answer to that one question still eluded me.

I know that if my parents had been able to answer that question for me, they would have. All through my childhood they gave to me, my brother, and my sister the very best they had to give. They truly loved and delighted in us, and in each other, and that kind of love is powerful. We knew that we were cherished.

Although my parents didn't know Jesus Christ personally, His "fingerprints" were all around us. We were always taught right from wrong and my parents modeled integrity. My father was transferred a number of times, and in each new place he made it a priority to find a church for us to attend. The church doctrine was probably less important to my dad than the people, the youth groups, and the positive and warm environment it would provide for us as children.

But none of those churches provided the answer to my question, so I was driven to look for it on my own. As a freshman in college I decided to minor in philosophy, thinking that surely the great thinkers down through the ages would be able to impart a real understanding of who God is. Unfortunately, the more I studied philosophy, the more confusing things became. Each one of these "great thinkers" had a different slant on the issues of knowledge, absolute truth, and the nature or even existence of God. Since even they couldn't reach a consensus, I came to the conclusion that possibly I could never really know truth either. But I kept seeking.

Having been disillusioned with the philosophers, I decided to approach the minister in our church. He was in charge of our youth group and had really touched my life, so I truly appreciated and admired him. But I later realized that he couldn't give me what he didn't have.

Going to him one day, I asked point blank, "Who is God? Who do you believe in?"

He answered, "That's easy. You just read the Bible, and what you want, you take. What you don't want, you throw out. Create your own theology."

I greatly respected this man, but it didn't take a great deal of discernment, even at age 18, for me to conclude that this was the *dumbest* advice I had ever been given. So between my pastor and the great philosophers of history, I was nowhere closer to finding truth than when I started. In fact, I felt farther away.

Still searching, I carefully watched other people and tried to find out what they believed. On the many flights between my home in Massachusetts and school in Illinois, I always hoped I would sit next to someone on the plane who knew God so they could explain Him to me. But I never did.

The Answer

It wasn't until my senior year in college that I finally found someone who seemed to have answers. There was a girl with Campus Crusade for Christ whom I had met several times, and I was always impressed with her. But even then, I thought she was just unique and I still didn't think that her answers would apply to me personally or address my questions. Yet I was intrigued and continued to follow her around out of curiosity.

After we had met a number of times, this girl invited me to a retreat in Chicago. I wasn't particularly enthusiastic about going, but she enticed me with the promise that we would go shopping in Chicago after the retreat. That was an offer I couldn't refuse.

I have learned over the years that God's purposes are intricately connected to His timing. That weekend at the retreat, after years of searching, my life was dramatically transformed.

Meeting and talking with lots of kids my age, I became convinced that they really did know who God was and that they even knew Him personally. When they explained to me that I could know God through Jesus Christ, I was totally flabbergasted. I knew that I had found the answer!

It was as though a light bulb went on. I committed my life to Christ that weekend and from then on everything began to change. Not long after that I went home and shared with my family about my experience and my new relationship with Christ. I'll never forget the gratitude I felt as, over time and one by one, my parents, my brother, and my sister all came to know Christ.

Because of my own experience, I really had a heart for university women, many of whom, like me, were seeking but not finding. So after graduating from college, I joined the staff of Campus Crusade for Christ. During my first year of training, I was surrounded by people who modeled the Christian life for me. Everything made so much sense and was becoming so clear to me that I just couldn't get enough; I was eager to join every Bible study and action group I could find. And to prepare me for working on college campuses, the Crusade staff trained me in sharing my faith with others in all kinds of situations. It was a wonderful way to begin my new life.

Making Choices

Then came the letter. I was dating a young man I had met in high school, and our relationship had become rather serious. We had gone together on and off for years and we had dreamed of becoming engaged sometime in the near future. I cared for him a great deal.

Friends and staff members in Campus Crusade began to lovingly share with me God's directive about not being "unequally yoked" with a non-believer. I knew they were right, so I started writing letters to this young man, sharing my faith with him and hoping with all my heart that he would come to embrace my same beliefs. But when he wrote back, he simply said "I don't see anything wrong with this God stuff, but I think you've gone overboard."

I was heartbroken.

I had to make a choice. As much as I cared for this man, I knew that God is who He says He is, and I believed Him. I believed His word and the loving principles I was learning in Scripture. He was already beginning to do some amazing things in my life and I didn't want to turn back. So I decided that, as an act of my will and not as an act of my emotions, I would choose to believe God and break off the relationship.

Since he was overseas at the time, the only way we could communicate was by letter. So I sat down and wrote the most difficult letter of my life and placed it in the mailbox that day on my way to class.

I knew, both intellectually and in my heart, that I had made the right choice. But there were still times afterward that doubts would creep in. Did I really blow it? Did I just destroy the best relationship that I might ever have in my life? In spite of the struggle, I understood better with each passing day that God is faithful, and I knew He had a purpose.

If I hadn't obeyed God at that point in my life, I never would have met Josh McDowell.

The Man of My Dreams

During my first year on staff with Campus Crusade, I shared an apartment with three other staff women. We made a "deal" at the first of the year that regardless of our schedules and the demands on our time, we would always meet back at the apartment and have dinner together. I was the youngest staff member and the newest Christian, so I felt like I hardly knew anything. But I knew that I wanted to spend my dinner hour with these mature believers who encouraged me in my faith.

During one particular meal the conversation turned to dating and we started talking about the types of men we liked to go out with. I reasoned that if you were going to go on record with something that important, you might as well be specific. So I spelled it out. I would be intrigued by a man who was very outgoing, who was interested in politics, could talk on any level, and who was very enthusiastic. I said that I really wanted to marry a radical for Jesus Christ. Then I boldly continued that I was normally attracted to men who were about 5'9" and who had dark hair and blue eyes. And just for good measure, I threw in that I was intrigued by people who were left-handed.

When I finished my list, one of my roommates responded with, "Hey, you know who we should get her together with?"

I was quick to ask, "Who?" and she answered, "Josh McDowell." I had never heard the name before and I had no idea who he was. But he is the one she thought of when I described the man of my dreams.

It wouldn't be long before I found out who Josh McDowell was. But it would take a lot longer for Josh McDowell to find out who *I* was!

The Speaker

That first year with Campus Crusade, I was assigned to the University of Texas in Austin. I finally heard Josh McDowell speak for the first time when he was invited to the campus to head up a number of rallies. Before that he had been traveling in Latin America and had been out of the country for some time, but his reputation had preceded him. I had heard that he was an amazing speaker. Listening to him, my first thought was, *Wow! I want to marry someone just like this man. He's exactly what I'm looking for.*

The same thing happened a few months later when I heard him speak at Arrowhead Springs in California. He was teaching high school kids on the subjects of love, sex, dating, and marriage. Sitting in the amphitheater after he finished, I closed my eyes, bowed my head, and prayed, "Lord, these principles make so much sense. I pray you'll give me a husband who believes these same things."

I wasn't praying, "Give me the speaker." I just wanted a husband who thought and believed *like* the speaker. But each time I heard Josh McDowell, listened to his views, and witnessed his passion for Christ, I became more and more attracted to him.

I Don't Believe We've Met . . .

There was a slight problem. After meeting Josh six or seven different times through Campus Crusade, he never had the slightest idea who I was. Each time we met in these different settings, he would graciously reach out his hand and say, "Hi, I don't believe we've met, but my name's Josh."

I would dejectedly think to myself, *I know who you are*

and yes, we have met. It was a bit humiliating.

My frustration didn't keep me from thinking that he was the most incredible speaker I had ever heard, and I was captivated by him. I used to quote him often, and when I heard that he was coming back to the University of Texas, I took all the girls in my Bible study and in my Action group to hear him. He spoke to a crowd of about 1,000 on a free speech platform on the steps of the Student Union. I sat on the grass way in the back, with my little group of students around me.

Suddenly, in the middle of his speech, he stopped, pointed to the back of the crowd, and said, "You out there in the bright-colored dress. Are you a Christian?"

I looked around, thinking *Who on earth is he talking to, pointing out in the audience?* Then I realized, to my astonishment, that I had on a bright-colored dress. He was looking at me. And so was everybody else.

Then he said, "Come on up here and share your testimony."

I would have been surprised if *anyone* had asked me to do that, but coming from him, I was stunned. I stood up and walked forward, and my legs were like jelly on springs.

Now my Campus Crusade for Christ training had always prepared us for opportunities just like this one. As staff members, we each wrote and memorized a three-minute testimony so that we would be ready to share it in any given situation. Unfortunately, everything I had memorized went right out the window. I couldn't even remember how to start.

All I could think to do was to share why Christ is important to me and how He had changed my life. After I finished, Josh came up to me and said, "Gee, that was really great. But it was six and a half minutes!"

I wanted to tell him, "Look, you're lucky that I didn't faint up there!" But I didn't.

After I sat back down, I was left wondering, *Why did he do that?* As a staff member, I knew that there were always

people with 30-second testimonies standing by to back up the speaker, to show solidarity for what he was saying. He certainly didn't need mine. How did he know I was a Christian? Why did he pick me out of a crowd of 1,000 students? The next day, he left to continue on his tour. And I was more intrigued than ever.

Several days later I was called into the office of the campus director of Campus Crusade. His first question was, "Dottie, have you gotten any long-distance phone calls lately?" When I said no and asked him why, he said with a twinkle in his eyes, "Never mind."

I certainly wasn't going to let that one slide, so I said, "Walter, tell me why you asked me that question!" He went on to explain that Josh McDowell had called to finish up business with the Central Texas District, and he had asked some questions about me. He wanted to know my name, who I was, and if I was dating anyone. Then, Walter said he mentioned that he might give me a call sometime.

I was astounded. As I walked out of the room, I vowed that I wasn't going to tell anyone what had happened, in case he didn't call. Nevertheless, whenever the phone rang I was right on top of it. But he never called.

Of course, Josh knew things that I didn't know. The day he called me out of the crowd to give my testimony, he was really just trying to think up an "innovative" way to meet me. The crowd was so large, he reasoned that once the meeting broke up he wouldn't be able to find me. So the best he could come up with was just to call me up onto the platform.

After he heard my testimony, Josh made a pact with the Lord. He committed that, although he was very interested in the girl in the bright-colored dress, he wasn't going to pursue me unless the Lord opened the door. And he left it there.

Operation Alternative

All of this took place early in 1970, when there was a great deal happening on college campuses across the country. At one

128

point, we got word that a group of radicals was planning to come take the University of Texas by storm, threatening to use violence in disrupting campus activities.

Campus Crusade responded by organizing "Operation Alternative." We wanted to take a bold stand, and send a message to the university, the community, and the media that there was an alternative to the radicals' approach. Five hundred staff members and students came from Texas, Alabama, Arkansas, and Oklahoma to march for Jesus Christ and to stand up against the message of the radicals. And the person who was called in to head up the rally was Josh McDowell.

In the midst of all the planning and organizing, I couldn't help but be excited that he was coming back. At the same time, I remembered the conversation I had with my director, and I never knew why Josh hadn't called. There was still a big question mark.

The rally was scheduled to kick off at one of the huge churches in Austin. Just before it started, I ran into a close friend of mine who had come in with Campus Crusade from Oklahoma, and we decided to sneak off for a 15-minute break over coffee. As we were catching up on several months of having been apart, she casually announced, "Guess who my roommate's dating?" When I asked who, she said "Josh McDowell."

My heart sank. "Really?" I said, trying to sound upbeat. "Do you think it's serious?"

She responded that it probably was serious, and that he had called her three times in the last month. *Oh well*, I thought. *So much for that idea.* Adding to the problem was the fact that I knew this girl's roommate and she was really, *really* cute. In fact, she was a knockout! That made the whole situation even more formidable.

Keeping my chin up, I went over to the church where the rally was about to start. There were kids everywhere who wanted to make an impression for Jesus Christ on that

campus, and the excitement was almost tangible.

I hadn't seen Josh face to face, but I did see him come in through one of the side doors. Then I spotted "the roommate" and I watched as their eyes met. The drama was right out of a movie script as I watched them move closer and closer to each other across the crowded floor. Then when they finally reached each other, I held my breath as they reached out and *shook hands*. I was elated! There's hope — all was not lost!

All in God's Time

The rest of the weekend, more important things took precedent. Everywhere you went students were sharing Christ with other students. It was amazing. Even though I didn't see Josh, I hadn't had time to think about it because we were so caught up in Operation Alternative. Only at the end, when I was standing by our book table and waiting to go home, did I notice him walking toward me.

"Gee, hi. Do you remember me?" he asked. That was a switch.

"I was just wondering if by any remote chance you're free tonight and might like to go out to dinner and a movie?"

My heart was racing, but I had to stay "cool." I told him that sounded great, then I went home and tried on every outfit I owned, and every outfit that all three of my roommates owned. Then I started getting nervous.

I started thinking about how I was such a new Christian and he was such a mature Christian. What if he started asking me about the Arab/Israeli crisis or the doctrine of reconciliation, or some other complicated biblical theme? As I was becoming more terrified, it finally occurred to me that this was someone I had admired from a distance for a very long time. I just decided to go out with him, be myself, see what I could learn, and have a good time. And if I never saw him again, it would be okay.

We went to dinner and saw the movie, *It's a Mad, Mad, Mad, Mad World,* and we had the most amazing, wonderful time. He didn't ask me about the Arab/Israeli crisis, or any other deep theological questions. We shared a magical time getting to know each other, and within two and a half months we were engaged. Just four months later, I became Mrs. Josh McDowell.

I know now that one of the things that played such a significant part in our relationship was God's timing. In any relationship where God is drawing two people together, there's the right person and there's the right timing. Even though God was bringing us together, there was a time to wait. He was leading Josh back from Latin America to establish a ministry in the United States. And because I was such a new believer, He was buying me time so that I could grow spiritually. All those times we met, it was as though Josh had blinders on, and he never saw me. But in the fullness of His time, in a crowd of a thousand, God took the blinders off and Josh asked me to come forward. And then it started.

What Is a Mrs. Josh McDowell?

The first thing I really had to deal with as a new bride was my own self-perception. I was still such a new Christian, and all of a sudden I was married to this dynamic man who was already becoming quite well-known. Josh was getting his ministry established in the States, as well as in some of the Latin countries. Everywhere we went, I began to wonder what my role should be. Should I be leading Bible studies or speaking, or be ever ready with pearls of wisdom? Should I be writing books? I didn't know what a Mrs. Josh McDowell was supposed to do, and I wasn't sure what people expected of me. I didn't know how to be me anymore, and I really longed to talk with someone in a similar position. I wanted to ask, "How do I know who I am now and what I'm supposed to do?"

The pressure never came from Josh, it was all coming from within me. But it was building, and it haunted me more and more. I found myself withdrawing a bit and afraid to be the spontaneous me that I had been. Finally, after struggling for a long time, I realized that God and Josh both loved me just the way I was. God knew that I was a young believer when He gave me to Josh, and He had a reason. I found at last that I was able to just be myself and rest in that. I didn't have to be a speaker or writer. It was okay that underneath Mrs. Josh McDowell there was just me, and I could be exactly who God made me. It was very freeing!

My Role

Once I came to terms with that question, I was able to move on to something powerful and of great consequence that I felt God wanted me to do, and I poured my life into it. I strongly felt that He wanted me to raise our children, to love them, and to be there with them when Josh couldn't always be there physically. And He had prepared me for that role many years before. From the time that I was a little girl my mother had impressed on me many times over how much she loved being a wife and a mother. In her eyes, there was no greater calling, and she used every opportunity to creatively express her delight in that. To her, motherhood was a great privilege and the most worthwhile calling, and her life testified to that throughout my childhood.

The seed that my mother planted was firmly rooted; I wanted to be a wife and a mom. And that desire was an integral part of God's design for our marriage. Josh is very strong and articulate, he's very gifted and capable, and he likes being on the front lines. But I like working backstage. I love being a cheerleader for my kids, my husband, my friends. It's a thrill for me to know that I am supporting someone who's doing mighty things. That's where I'm comfortable. That's where I prefer to be.

I know that I have an incredible advantage because I was loved and cherished as a child, and I have a husband who loves and cherishes me. I have known from the beginning that I was never in competition with Josh's ministry. Our family is his ministry. He ministers to us and then we minister together. I think Josh is an amazing speaker, and even more, an amazing person. He's just an exciting man to live with, and there's never a dull moment around our house. I love the new ideas and new visions that Josh is always coming up with, and I love the passion he has to reach out to people and to make an impact in the world for Christ.

Josh didn't share my idyllic background. His father was an alcoholic and that made life very difficult for him as he was growing up. He tells that painful story in his testimony, and after speaking one day he was approached by a group of people. They wanted to share with him some things they had learned about being adult children of alcoholic parents. Up until that point, it had never occurred to Josh that there are certain characteristics and problems that are unique to these adult children of alcoholics.

It's very common for an adult child of an alcoholic to be a rescuer, because that's what they had to do as a child. Josh tried to rescue everyone. As I saw him do that, I used to think he was the most generous person I'd ever met. But we learned that part of that was under compulsion, he *had* to rescue people. It was painful to have to deal with those issues, but it also helped him to know that other people had dealt with the same things, and they understood how he felt. And when he began to understand and get a handle on some of those things, it freed him to be able to make choices. It was a hard time, but I know that God used it to minister to Josh and to help mend a heart that had once been broken.

As Josh traveled so extensively with his ministry, it was important to both of us for me to be home raising our children. Josh is passionate about his family and the love he has for his children, so I know that what I am doing is more valuable to him, and to us, than all the other engagements and commitments I might have had. In our home and in our ministry, God designed the two of us to complement each other. I'm very grateful and awed by God's wisdom.

That's not to say that there aren't times when family life can be exasperating or frustrating. I would worry about any mom who says it's all a bed of roses, because there are times when it's really baffling and/or exhausting. But I can't imagine anything more fulfilling.

I recently came across a verse that just made my heart sing: "I have no greater joy than to hear that my children are walking in the truth" (3 John 4).

We have four children, one who just graduated from college, one who is a senior in college, a daughter who's a senior in high school, and our little one who's in the sixth grade. As they have grown, I have learned that there is no greater joy than to see your kids making right choices and following the Lord. That, to me, is far more valuable than a career or any commitment that would lure me away from my family. As I watch my children making wise choices, I can taste the fruit of all the many, many years I've invested in being a mom. The reward is enormous and I remain grateful for my mother's example.

Now that our children are older, I have found that the demands on my time are changing. Since we don't have toddlers anymore, I have more time to work with Josh. Although I'm not an official editor, I really enjoy working with words, so it's been fun editing a lot of his material behind the scenes. He and I have written some children's books together and we're currently working on a children's Bible story book. Although we walk through many different seasons in life, I want my primary focus to always be my husband and my children.

Thirsting for God

Since we're so close, when my children do experience trials, my heart aches with them. When we moved to our home in Texas just over two years ago, one of my daughters had an extremely difficult time making the transition. She truly grieved over the situation, and my heart mourned for her. I knew God had brought us here and that it was His best. I wanted her to feel the same way, but she just couldn't get past the hurt.

It's so interesting how many times, when we come alongside other people who are hurting, God begins to really work in our own lives. Two years ago, I felt like I had a good solid relationship with the Lord. But as I watched my daughter suffer through such terrible unhappiness, I found myself falling on my knees, asking for wisdom. I had to rely on Him in a different way, and I thirsted for His word.

Before that time I studied the Bible through the "hopscotch" method. (You probably won't find that one in seminary class.) I would move around in the Bible, reading a little of this and a little of that, without a whole lot of continuity. It was sincere, and I learned good things, but it was more of an intellectual approach than a real searching of heart, mind, and soul.

But the pain of watching my child suffer caused me to become desperate for God's Word, and I thirsted for it like a man in a desert. I mapped out a systematic plan of study that covered the entire Bible. And it all became new. It was all so relevant to me, it washed me from the inside out. Scripture gave me hope, it gave me courage, and it gave me answers to things I had never before understood.

In retrospect, I'm so grateful for that very dark time. My daughter finally got through the pain. She was warmly embraced by the kids in her new school, and she's now president of the Student Council, co-editor of the yearbook, and playing varsity basketball. In spite of the pain and hurt, she knows that this is where she's supposed to be. Throughout these two long years, God has taught her mighty things. But even more than that, He used this time in our lives to bring me to a new place, and to teach me things I never could have imagined.

Just One Book

I love the verse in 2 Timothy 3:16. It begins, "All Scripture is God-breathed. . . ." On first reading that verse, it had a profound effect on me and I've never forgotten it. If Scripture is God-breathed, then everything in Scripture is true and it relates directly to me. Everything.

That concept is all the more precious to me because of my earlier search for truth through philosophy. There were so many different lines of thought, I remember wishing that there was just a book, just one simple book that would tell me what truth was. I vowed that, if there was such a book, I would commit myself to it. But in my futile search, I became skeptical and frustrated.

As a new Christian, when I discovered the Bible the light went on. There really *is* a book, and it tells me who God is and how I should live my life. Now, whenever I read the Bible, I pause to remember that "All Scripture is God-breathed." That is all the encouragement I need to know that whatever happens, whatever crumbles around me, the Word of God never changes. And the certainty of that keeps me going.

Last year, I did a study on standing firm. I kept coming across those words in the Bible, and I wanted to dig deeper. So with my fledgling computer skills and the help of my highly computer-literate 11-year-old daughter, I sought out all the verses I could find on "standing firm." Throughout Scripture, the Lord tells us in many different ways that there are tremendous benefits to be realized if we will stand firm in Him, regardless of our circumstances. And that has gripped me.

Standing firm is an act of the will. Sometimes our emotions go along with it, and sometimes they don't, but it's a choice. Making choices and communicating those choices to our children is critical. Every time we do something in life, we're making choices, every day, all day long. And every choice has an implication.

Many years ago, I made a choice to marry a radical for Jesus Christ, and I am so grateful for the life that God has given us. Because of His love toward us, I have learned what it means to stand firm, and I know what it is to love with abandon.

Dottie McDowell

For more information contact:
        Josh McDowell Ministries
        660 International Pkwy, Suite 100
        Richardson, TX 75081
        (972) 907-1000

Darlene Ankerberg

Darlene is married to Christian television show host and evangelist John Ankerberg. She is actively involved on a full-time basis in the operation of their television ministry, headquartered in Chattanooga, Tennessee. In addition, she travels extensively with her husband and assists him in meeting the demands of numerous personal appearances and speaking engagements. She is also the mother of Michelle, who is currently enrolled in Bob Jones University.

Chapter 7

In an effort to prevent terrorist attacks, armor-plated tanks escorted the planes along the runway with their mounted machine guns pointed out into the bush. In light of the situation, we just didn't see any way we could get a significant number of people to attend a crusade meeting in the city.

I know that we have an enemy. He's alive and well, and even though he stands against everything we stand for, it's exciting to realize that he is no match for Jesus Christ and the work that He is accomplishing through all of us.

One of my first insights into this spiritual battle came on a winter night a number of years ago. My husband, John, and I were traveling from Chicago to Connecticut to attend a very important meeting. It was bitterly cold and a blinding snow was blowing across the highway, enveloping everything in a white haze.

Without warning, we hit a slick patch of icy road, and losing control of the car we slid down an embankment and landed against a wall of snow. Within just a few minutes a patrolman arrived on the scene and checked us out. Once he determined that we were okay, he left us there while he went back to call for a tow truck.

John and I were still huddled in the car when we suddenly realized with a sense of horror that an 18-wheel tractor trailer had made the same mistake we had and was barreling straight down the embankment on top of us. The driver managed to maneuver the cab of the truck past us, but the truck bed came crashing down on top of our car, crushing the roof down to the top of the seats.

I closed my eyes and fully believed I was on my way to heaven, but I opened them again when I heard John urging me to hurry and get out of the car. He was afraid the huge weight of the truck was going to keep pressing down on top of the car until it crushed us. The snow was so high I couldn't get the door open on my side and John's side was blocked by the truck, so we crawled through the window into the deep snowbank. The terrified truck driver made his way around to where we were, expecting the worst. Miraculously, we both escaped without any serious injuries.

Looking back, I know that car wreck was Satan's attempt to destroy us and our ministry. Since then, I've watched many times over the years as the enemy has attacked at critical points in our work, or just before God initiated something new. But it has been so exciting to see that, in every case, God has protected us and proven His faithfulness. It doesn't mean that hard things won't happen, but I have learned that we can trust Him in every situation.

She Was Always There

I don't think I would ever have learned to trust God the way I do if it hadn't been for my grandmother. My dad was an evangelist and he traveled all over the United States and overseas. In those days, people didn't travel by jet planes, so when my parents left for places like Australia, they were often gone for months at a time. Our family lived on a farm in Indiana with my grandmother and great-grandmother. I loved my parents and was grateful for the kind of work they were in, but my heart will always hold a special place for my grandmother. She is the one who was always there; the one who prayed for me, taught me, encouraged me, and for all practical purposes, raised me.

Darlene Ankerberg

I know firsthand the tremendous impact that grandparents can have in the lives of their grandchildren. My grandmother prayed for me every single day, and when I went away to college she never missed a day in sending me a letter. Every time I went to the mailbox her handwritten note would be there, always encouraging me to seek the Lord's direction, always with a verse or two that was special to her. I think her favorite was Proverbs 3:5–6:

> Trust in the Lord with all your heart, And do not lean on your own understanding. In all your ways acknowledge Him, And He will make your paths straight.

Because of my grandmother, the idea of trusting God, depending on Him, and believing He would guide my paths was ingrained in my heart and mind from the very earliest years. For that, I am deeply indebted to her.

Making It Mine

Near our farm in Indiana there was a little country church we attended faithfully, and that is where I gave my life to the Lord when I was seven years old. I was enrolled in vacation Bible school, and on this one particular day we all paraded into the church as usual and I was given the singular honor of carrying the Bible. As I listened to the speaker that day explain what it meant to have the Lord as your personal Savior, I decided that was something I was probably going to have to do for myself. Even though I had heard my father teach the very same thing, I realized that day I wasn't going to get to heaven just because my father was a minister. So as I sat there on the very first row, with that big black Bible in my lap, I bowed my head and asked the Lord Jesus Christ to come into my heart.

The Right Person

Even as far back as junior high school, I had prayed that God would lead me to the right person whom He had for me

to marry. But in the summer between my junior and senior years in college, my prayers were put to the test.

When my parents weren't traveling, they lived in Boca Raton, Florida, where they were associated with a Bible conference that was held there. After my junior year at Bob Jones University, I went home to Boca to join them for the summer. My first week home, a boy whom I had dated at school came down and asked me to marry him. I didn't give him an answer, but told him I needed to pray and think about it.

Deep down, I harbored a lot of doubts. I knew that I was independent and I had some clear goals in mind, and it just seemed as if I was in too much of a leadership role in this relationship. I wanted what God wanted, and I believed that God would want me to have a husband who would lead me spiritually. So I waited.

One Wednesday night I attended a prayer meeting at our church. Walking in the back of the room, I saw a family sitting there — *somebody new*! That was exciting because Boca Raton had a lot of retired people and when you were just 19 or 20, any new person who didn't have gray hair really caught your attention. We had gotten there late and there was nowhere left to sit but the front row. I sat through the whole meeting wondering who the people were in the back of the church.

As it turned out, the people in the back of the church were friends of my parents. The couple had known my mom and dad back at Winona Lake, Indiana, when Youth for Christ was just getting started. Along with Youth for Christ, Billy Graham was just beginning his ministry, and they had been involved in that as well. So I was introduced to Mr. and Mrs. Ankerberg, and to their daughters, and to their son John.

Visiting from Chicago, they told us they had really enjoyed going to the beach while they were in Boca. I immediately pointed out that they had gone to the *wrong* beach, and I knew a much better one, and I would be *glad* to take them there!

The next night, John asked me out for dinner. By the end

of the night, when I returned home, I knew that God had answered my prayer and led me to the man I was going to marry. I went in, sat down, and wrote a heartfelt letter of farewell to the boy who had asked me to marry him.

John and I dated every day until my family had to leave to go up north to Bible conferences for the rest of the summer. Then I went back to school in South Carolina and he went back to Illinois and we kept up a long distance relationship, seeing each other whenever we could. There were very large phone bills and *very* long letters, and then I graduated.

I had already been accepted to work on my master's degree and my father really wanted me to pursue that, so John and I dated for four years. But as soon as I finished my graduate work, we were married and moved to Chicago where John was enrolled in seminary.

The Last Class of the Day

The Lord had an interesting assignment for me while we were in Chicago, one that I'll never forget. I got a job in two different suburbs of the city teaching junior high school kids. We didn't have the same kind of problems that we have today, but many of these kids were from broken homes and they had their own set of problems to deal with. I really wanted to be a witness to those children.

One of my classes was a group of eighth grade boys who were assigned to me for remedial reading. They were kind of the "problem" kids in the school and the principal kept them separated except for my class, where they were all grouped together. It was the last class of the day, just after gym, and by the time they got to me, they usually had already been at each other's throats.

I took the class on one condition. I told the principal that he or the assistant principal had to be present somewhere in the building at all times during my class, and that if I buzzed their office, they were to *get down there fast!* As it turned out, there were a number of fights, but since most of the boys were bigger than I was, I decided not to risk life and limb trying to break them up!

But there were also some very special times in that reading class. I wanted those boys to see something in my life that was different. They knew my husband was a minister and although that was something new for them, they were also intrigued in a way. There were times that we started talking about "life" and never even got to the reading lesson. But I had a chance to impart something to those boys.

As I look back now, I believe that the Lord had me specifically in that place at that time for a reason. And I often wonder what happened to those five boys who spent the last hour of each school day sitting (or fighting) in my classroom.

Overseas

Like me, John had always traveled in evangelistic work with his dad, even through high school and college. So it seemed natural for us to continue traveling to faraway places to share the gospel. Not long after we were married we spent two and a half months conducting meetings and working with missionaries in the Orient — Taiwan, Japan, and the Philippines. We both had a heart for missions, and after John finished seminary we started receiving a number of invitations to travel to other countries. Many of the invitations were from Africa, and one of those meetings turned out to be especially significant.

In April of 1977 we were asked to come do a citywide crusade in Salisbury (now Harare), Rhodesia, which is now Zimbabwe. But before the crusade could actually take place, we had to go over for a setup meeting to make all the arrangements.

On our arrival, we were discouraged to find that the country was virtually paralyzed by an ongoing state of guerrilla warfare. Curfews forced almost everyone to stay home, and travel was slow and dangerous because there were bombs in the streets. Security checkpoints were everywhere, and at the airport planes were subject to terrorist attacks during takeoffs and landings. In an effort to prevent these attacks, armor-plated tanks escorted the planes along the runway with their mounted machine guns pointed out into the bush. In light of the situation, we just didn't see any way we could get a significant number of people to attend a crusade meeting in the city.

One day we were traveling through Salisbury and John noticed a large building that had just been constructed. He casually asked the man who was in charge of the crusade what the building was, and the man answered that it was their new sports arena.

John immediately thought of an idea. Stopping the car, he found the man who was in charge of the building. While giving John a tour, the man pointed out that the entire building was wired for television so that major sports events could be aired nationwide. To John, this "sports arena" seemed like a perfect place to hold a crusade.

We knew that all of the television in the country was under the control of a government agency. John contemplated the situation for a long time. Then one night he woke up sensing that the Lord was encouraging him with a plan. He decided to act on his convictions.

John set up a meeting with the gentleman who was in charge of the television agency and explained his idea to him. This government secretary listened as John told him that we wanted to conduct a crusade and that we wanted to reach as many people as possible. Then John asked him point blank, "Would it be possible for our team to address the nation via television?"

The secretary answered, "You know, here in Rhodesia we have a national policy that anything associated with religion is free."

The Lord had opened a huge door!

We brought in kids from all the schools in the area and

put on a large youth conference. In addition, we were given time on nationwide television to present the gospel directly to the people of Rhodesia. Working closely with the missionaries from the area, we all marveled as we watched the Lord move in a powerful way in the very midst of a country being torn apart by war.

Airwaves

For John and me, the trip to Rhodesia was the beginning of something bigger. For the first time, we began to think seriously about television as an incredible resource that God could use to expand the message of the gospel far beyond the walls of a meeting room.

John has always been passionate in his defense of biblical truth, and television was soon going to provide him with a larger "stage" on which to present that truth to people everywhere.

A seed had been planted, and the idea of a televised ministry was never far from our thoughts. My father encouraged John along those same lines, believing that television would be a powerful tool in the future and that John's style would adapt especially well to it. But in the meantime, we continued to travel with crusades and missionary groups, spending two or three months of every year overseas.

It's interesting to me how God often brings other people into our lives to help "push" us in the right direction. Over the years, we had become good friends with a couple who lived in Kansas City. They had a ministry to teens, and John had often spoken at their rallies, conferences, and teen ranches.

One day the husband, Al, called John. He felt that the Lord was leading him to start a television station and he wanted John to put together a program. It was an exciting opportunity! John envisioned a format where people with opposing points of view would be engaged in discussions on the program.

Once he committed to the show, John would fly out there

on weekends, do the programs, and then return to our normal schedule of evangelistic meetings. But the workload was overwhelming. One weekend, he taped 40 programs and had to do extensive research for each one.

The Lord had a better way. He seemed to say to John, "You know, there are a lot of gifted men and women who have been involved in these cults, or who have invested years of study. Why don't you have them come on the program, and you just ask the questions?"

That was the real beginning of the show, and it all started in Kansas City. But about that same time, CBN, the Christian Broadcasting Network, was also getting underway. John met with the man who was doing all the programming for the Family Channel, CBN, and they accepted our program. We also forwarded a tape to a station in Chicago, and they accepted it as well.

Crossroads

As more and more of our time was being placed in the television ministry, it left us less time for our traveling evangelistic work. Also, now our daughter Michelle was two and a half years old, and all of a sudden, things were changing. In addition, a tremendous amount of our funds was going into the television programs. Even though the mail was coming in faster than we could answer it, there was still a great deal more money going out than coming in. Over and over, my thoughts were, *Here we are, Lord. What are we supposed to do?*

It was becoming increasingly difficult to live in one place while having to travel every week to another place to do the show. About that time, John's dad received a request from a gentleman he knew named Dr. Spiros Zodhiates. Dr. Zodhiates had a worldwide missionary organization that was based in Chattanooga, Tennessee. Their headquarters in Chattanooga included a fully equipped television studio.

Dr. Zodhiates' brother had just passed away, and he was concerned about the ministry and who would take it over if something happened to him as well. So he called John's dad and asked him if he had any suggestions. John's dad just happened to know of a young television preacher in need of a studio and television facilities.

John flew down and met with Dr. Zodhiates and everything seemed to fall in place. We were able to use the television facilities for the show, John helped Dr. Zodhiates with his ministry, and within a year the TV ministry just took off.

John was still traveling, but now it really became impossible for him to carry two full-time jobs. We felt the Lord was leading us to do the television on a full-time basis, so we committed everything toward that end, pulled up stakes in Chicago, and made the decision to live in Chattanooga.

Each one of the steps we've taken seemed huge at the time. We never knew if things were going to work out, if the ministry was going to be effective, or even if we were going to have a job from one day to the next!

Walking by Faith

Leaving Chicago, we left virtually everything and everyone we knew behind. Looking at the financial requirements in front of us, the numbers seemed staggering. I'll never forget the first time we received a check for $1,000 in the mail from someone who had seen our program. Television was relatively new then, so for someone to send a check of that amount to help support a ministry was impressive. But it was hardly a "secure" situation. We were totally dependent on the Lord.

Television is a very expensive endeavor, and it's a hard thing to gauge. When we were able to add new stations, we went through periods of growth and expansion. But the overhead is enormous, and we never knew if a new station was going to pay for itself until we were already several months into our commitment. And even though we were a ministry, John and I had to sign personally for everything we did.

Those can be hard times. But they are also good times because that's when we have to totally trust the Lord, and He has always been faithful. It's one thing to trust the Lord when we think we have some degree of control and we can still manipulate our circumstances. It's another thing to trust Him when there is absolutely nothing else that can be done. To me, that's the most exciting thing in my Christian life. The most thrilling is to know that when I can't do one human thing possible, that's when the Lord takes over. That's *total* dependence on Him.

Not too long ago, the Lord gave me an opportunity to put those convictions to the test. After 15 years on the Family Channel, we suddenly and unexpectedly lost our airtime when the Family Channel was sold to Robert Murdoch and Fox for $1.8 billion. It was something totally beyond our control, a decision that other people made. But it was a seeming blow to everything we were doing, and it was a hard thing to accept. The whole budget for our ministry was based on the contributions of the large audience of viewers from the Family Channel, and all of our future plans for outreach and expansion were tied into it. But with just a 30-day notice, everything changed.

We were suddenly completely cut off from our weekly audience of several million people. Messages came pouring in from people who said things like, "I came out of a cult because of this and now I can't even get your program," or just, "We miss your ministry so much." On one hand, it has been a heartbreaking thing for us. We were forced to let go nearly 100 people who worked with us answering phones and in administration. But we know that God has a reason for everything, and realizing that this was totally beyond our control, we once again were able to say, "Okay, Lord. It's all in Your hands."

As Christians, I think one of the most difficult things to understand is that even if something doesn't work out the way we want it to, it doesn't mean that we are not in the middle of God's will. Just because we fail doesn't make us a failure. Sometimes the hard thing — the best thing — is to persevere. Even when, for whatever reason, God doesn't allow things to work out as we want them to, it's important to keep trying. John and I are committed to serving the Lord, and we are doing everything we can to get the gospel out to a hurting world. But ultimately, it is all in God's hands. I find that very comforting.

This past winter we were faced with an entirely different kind of setback. Sometime around Christmas, John contracted a virus that we first thought was a flu bug. But it knocked him off his feet, and he just couldn't seem to shake it. The doctors are not completely sure what they're dealing with, but John was ill for most of the winter, and now, almost nine months later, he is still only about 80 percent of his full strength.

Apparently, God wanted us to remember that when we are weak, then He is strong. While John was fighting just to regain his strength, God was working out some exciting things in the ministry.

After almost three years we finally got some encouraging news! Because of the high cost, it has been almost impossible for our ministry to buy air time on major nationwide networks. But in the last 30 days, the floodgates seemed to have opened.

We were attending the Booksellers Convention when our media buyers called and said that a large network in the eastern part of the United States had invited us to be on their network of 13 million homes (26 million people). The time period was great, 7:30 to 8:00 p.m., right before Charles Stanley's "In Touch" program. But the cost for 52 weeks for this network was $100,000. John told the network he would feel a little more comfortable if we were able to raise half the money before we went on the air.

With "fear and trembling," we began to call a few folks about this project. One by one people encouraged us to take this opportunity. John wasn't feeling that well at the time and said that if any one of those people that we first called had turned him down, he would have dropped the entire idea. It just seemed like such a big mountain to climb.

But still, God seemed to be opening this door to us. To

make a long story short, one by one, 19 people committed to give $50,000 so that we could go on this network.

No sooner had this been accomplished than we received invitations to go on at 9:00 p.m. on Sunday night in Denver, Atlanta, and Orlando, all large television markets.

A week later a man came in from California to talk with John. We had no idea what he was going to say or why he was coming. When he arrived, we went out for lunch and he calmly explained that his company had bought 15 stations in different parts of the United States and wanted us to air our program on them!

All of these invitations came within a four to six-week period of time. The final opportunity was from a huge network of 50 million homes (reaching 100 million people) which was located in the top ten television markets in the United States. Incredibly they offered us 8:00 p.m. on Sunday night — all across America. It's an unbelievable opportunity, but it comes with a great responsibility. We're just trusting God to supply our needed response. In a very short period of time went from the deep valleys all the way to the top of the mountains. Again, we are just to hold on to God and let Him have His way.

Partnership

I've had many women come up to me over the years and say, "I could never work with my husband!" Next to the Lord, John is the most important person in my life, my best friend. I truly enjoy sharing the day-to-day grind with him. There has been great joy and great frustration, and I have to believe those things have drawn us closer.

John probably has greater highs and lows than I do. Since I'm an optimistic person by nature, I usually try to put a positive spin on every situation, to lighten things up a little. It's not that John is negative — he's probably just more realistic than I am! But I like to be an encourager, and I'm always looking for that silver lining.

There have been times when I've gotten a little *too*

involved in John's work. On one particular day, I watched with the studio audience as they were taping a segment of the show. The people who were opposing John were losing ground fast in their argument. After a few minutes, they really became incensed and started attacking John personally. When one of the men made a particularly insulting remark, I jumped to my feet, pointed to him, and blurted out, "THAT'S NOT TRUE!" There was a stunned silence for a few moments, and then John turned and looked at me incredulously, as if to say, "Who *is* this woman?" They had to edit me out.

When our only child, Michelle, left for college, John made the remark that he felt as if we were "dating" again. I think that's one of the keys to our marriage. We hold on to that excitement we felt when we first met. When I'm at home cooking dinner, I still love to hear the garage door go up; John is home. We find ways to spend time alone together, and ways to have fun. Most importantly, we talk, we communicate.

I know those things don't come easily in these times in which we live. When Michelle was little, there were days when my world seemed to revolve around her and her needs, and John's world seemed to revolve around the ministry. Then we would all wind up in the same house, with nothing to talk about! My heart goes out to mothers with babies and toddlers because those little ones have a way of controlling the days and the nights. But talking — just sharing with each other — is a wonderful way to stay close.

There is something else that I learned from my grandmother. She used to caution me over and over, "Don't ever let the sun go down on your wrath. Always get things settled before you lay your head on that pillow at night. Don't let things keep seething." That's one of the things I brought to our marriage, and it's a principle we always seek to follow. When problems are allowed to fester, there's a real danger of bitterness, and bitterness can be deadly.

Darlene Ankerberg

Coattails

When I was in high school, I fully committed my life to the Lord. I told Him that I wanted to serve Him, to live for Him, and that I would go wherever He wanted me to go. But growing up with evangelists for parents, and then marrying an evangelist, I sometimes felt as if I was just hanging onto everyone else's coattails.

I reached a point where I realized that I had to let go of those "coattails" and start allowing the Lord to direct me individually. Focusing on my own personal relationship with Him, one of the things that was impressed on me was that He wanted *me* to be a witness.

People have often come up to me with questions, expecting me to know everything that John knows. I don't have my husband's mind, and I often have to tell them, "I really don't know. You're going to have to ask him." But I have learned that, even though I don't have all the doctrinal answers, I do have the love of Christ, and that is mine to share.

Not long after God began to encourage me in this area, John and I were on a flight from Fort Lauderdale to Atlanta. There was a problem with the plane, so we were detained on the ground while they dealt with it.

John was seated by the window, I was in the middle seat, and a nice young man was seated next to me in the aisle seat. He and I started a polite conversation with the usual, "Where are you headed, and we're going to be a little late making connections," and so on. We eventually got around to the subject of the Bible, and he told me that he had just married a young woman who was Catholic. She was urging him to join the Catholic church, and he wanted to know what my thoughts were.

John was no help at all; he just sat there. Even though I knew he was listening, he never said a word. I quickly realized he wasn't going to bail me out on this one.

I jumped right in and started witnessing to him about

153

needing to have a personal relationship with the Lord. He listened and we talked, and before long we were saying our goodbyes in Atlanta.

Five years later, I received a letter from this young man and his wife. They wanted to tell me their story.

Apparently he returned home from that trip and told his wife about our conversation. She was extremely upset with me because, after talking with me, he had decided not to join the Catholic church. Even though she didn't know me and had never met me, she really didn't like me!

But the Lord was working. Through a number of different circumstances, they both came to realize that they didn't know the Lord personally. Once they understood, they turned their lives over to Him and got involved in a small church in New Jersey where they were living. They wanted to tell me that our conversation on the plane that day led to the beginning of what became their new life in Christ.

A few years later at a banquet in Philadelphia, John and I had the opportunity to see this young man again and to meet his wife and three children. It still brings tears to my eyes when I think about them. I'm not John, and I'm no Bible scholar. But just in sharing my heart with this one man, the Lord allowed me to watch as He did a tremendous thing in the life of their family.

That is the most stirring thing for me — to know that I'm not just swinging on someone else's spiritual coattails. I can love God and serve Him, right where I am. I now ask the Lord each day to lead me to someone so that I can just sow the seed. The privilege is mine, the outcome is His.

"Hurry Up, Mom. We've Got to Pray."

As I said, my heart always goes out to parents with young children. When we're raising them, it seems like the toughest, most complicated thing in the world! I don't think any of us are prepared in advance for what it means to bring up a child.

One of the first things our daughter Michelle had to learn was flexibility. Our home seems like a circus sometimes, and everything can change at the drop of a hat. People are always coming and going, and the telephone can ring at all hours of the day and night. But John and I made a commitment that we were never going to put the ministry before Michelle. I have always wanted her to be a part of everything we do, and never to resent it.

It's difficult, and sometimes it seems like a huge juggling act. As Michelle was growing up she watched how we handled difficult situations. We've always talked freely with her — we let her know about the good times, and we tell her about the hard times. She knows the things we pray about, and what it means to depend on the Lord.

When Michelle was younger, I used to "take her captive" in the car. Instead of putting her on the bus or using carpools, I always drove her to school, to piano lessons, to gymnastics, and to all the endless other places. We would talk about everything — boys, drugs, people I had dated, why Christians don't always act like Christians, whom she should date. Some of our best times together resulted from those hours when I had her "trapped" in the car.

Every morning, Michelle and I spent five or ten minutes together talking and praying before she went to school. John was on a different schedule, so he prayed with us at night, but the mornings were ours. For years, I would call to her to pray with me. But by the time she reached high school, she was usually the one who would call out, "Hurry up, Mom. We've got to pray." Those were wonderful times, and I miss them now that she's in college. But I have watched those seeds take root in her life, and I am so thankful that she loves the Lord and follows Him. I can't wait to see what God has for her!

First Things First

There is a definite order and sequence to our lives. Jesus said the greatest commandment is that we "love the Lord our God with all our heart and with all our soul and with all our mind" (Matt. 22:37). There is a reason why He put that

commandment first, because when we obey that, then all our priorities fall into place.

When I love God with all my heart, then I find myself drawn to His word, and spending time in prayer. I seek His protection and I constantly ask for wisdom. James 1:5 says, "If any of you lacks wisdom, let him ask of God," because He will give it to us.

There are so many little traps that we can fall into during the course of a day, things like selfish ambition, fear, and self-pity. But I have found that when I put God first, and continually go to Him, those things seem to fall away and He gives me all of the wisdom, strength, and peace that I need.

People have asked me, if I had my life to live over, would I do it any differently? The answer is no. There have been good times and hard times and frustration and discouragement, but I wouldn't change anything. My dependence is on the Lord, and I am confident in where He has brought me, and where He is taking me. It doesn't mean that life is easy — I don't understand why some people have to suffer from cancer and why others die so young. But I know that God is all-powerful and all-knowing and all-loving, and it's never too late for us to come to Him. He wants nothing more than to give us His best.

I don't know what our future holds, but whatever happens, I know the importance of keeping our lives in perspective. We're only here for a brief time, and the Lord has promised to give us all the strength and love we need in serving Him. I know with full assurance that if we will just depend on Him, He'll take us through each day, every step of the way. And for those of us who know Him as Savior, the very best is still ahead.

Elizabeth Newbold

Elizabeth Newbold was one of the most remarkable women I have ever met. She was a woman whose life flowed with the joy and radiance of our living Savior, who demonstrated through her life and ministry the dynamic power of the Holy Spirit. But even more important than the radiance which she communicated is the obvious impact of her spiritual life multiplied through the lives of her disciples.

Dr. Bill Bright, president and founder,
Campus Crusade for Christ

The above excerpt was taken from Dr. Bright's foreword to the book *Elizabeth, a Blessing to All Nations* written by Janie Buck.

Elizabeth went to be with her Lord in 1985, but before she did, her life, her joy, and her ministry powerfully impacted unknown numbers the world over. Indeed, the impact of her life is still being celebrated. This is her story, taken from her own testimony, summaries of events in her life, and excerpts from Mrs. Buck's book.

Chapter 8

*Jean said, "Do you believe that Christ died for
your sins?"*

*I said, "Well, of course. I'm knowledgeable. He
died for the sins of the world." Did she think I hadn't
even been to the Easter program?*

Her Story

It's always a joy for me to have the opportunity to share
how God has worked in my life. And He has *certainly* worked
in my life! I'll tell you, once you give Him an opportunity, He
really goes to work.

I'd like to just start back at the very beginning. I suppose
I could say that my life has been very much like a song that
Peggy Lee made popular in years gone by. It was called, "Is
That All There Is?"

It wasn't that life passed me by; I usually got what I
wanted. It's just that when I got what I wanted, it just didn't
seem to bring the fulfillment for which I was searching.

That's the way the song goes. She starts off by saying:

I always wanted to see a fire, and then one day
my house caught on fire. And my daddy took me out
across the street and we stood there together and we
watched the house burn down to the ground. And
halfway through, I said to myself, "You mean that's
all there is to a fire?"

And then when I was ten years old, my daddy

took me to a circus. I had always wanted to go to a circus. There I watched the women on the trapeze and the lions and the tigers and the elephants. But halfway through, I said to myself, "You mean, this is all there is to a circus?"

And when I was 16 years old, I fell in love. Oh, I met the most wonderful man. And we used to walk together, and look into each other's eyes and talk for hours. And then one day, he just went away. And I said to myself, "Do you mean, that's all there is to love?"

Well, if that's all there is, let's bring out the booze, let's have a ball if that's all. And somebody said to me, "Well if that's the way you feel about it, why don't you just end it all?"

No, I don't think I'm ready yet for that final disappointment, because I know when I draw my last breath, I'm going to ask myself the question, "Do you mean, that's all there is to life?"

I was well on down that road. That song expressed my experience of life. I was 35 years old before that great day when I met Christ and found there was meaning and purpose to life.

I was born in Tuscaloosa, Alabama. It was a great place to grow up, right in the backyard of the University of Alabama's Crimson Tide football team. One day I just *knew* I would grow up and date a member of the Crimson Tide football team. This was my first real goal. I did grow up and I actually *dated* a member of the Alabama football team. And halfway through the date, I asked myself the question, "Do you mean this is all there is to dating a member of the Alabama football team?"

And then disappointments and disappointments. The summer before my high school senior year, my parents decided to move to Birmingham, Alabama. Birmingham seemed much farther away from Tuscaloosa than it does now. I didn't know a soul in Birmingham. We moved in the summer and I didn't have the opportunity to meet anyone there. I only had one friend, the girl who lived in the house behind me. So I spent a lot of lonely hours wishing I was back in Tuscaloosa, and I went back every opportunity I had.

The Career

At this time I decided if life was ever going to have any meaning for me, I was going to have to really *do* something with my life. A career, perhaps. *That* would be it. Problem: I really didn't have any talent. But I listened to some radio programs and discovered you really didn't need a lot of talent to have a singing program on the air. So that became my goal.

One day, my friend who lived behind me phoned and said, "Hey, Elizabeth. I wish you'd come over. I have a friend who's visiting from Atlanta. She's going to be here for the weekend and I want you to meet her."

This was exciting. I rushed over to meet her friend who was a cute girl from Atlanta. The Atlanta friend said, "I hope you can stay for a little while, because in a few minutes my boyfriend is coming on the air. He has a singing program."

Immediately, my wheels started turning: "She lives in Atlanta. She has a boyfriend in Birmingham who has a radio program. I live in Birmingham. Isn't that interesting."

I stayed for the radio program and he was delightful. I remember thinking at the time, *If he looks anything like he sounds, she's really got something here.* My new Atlanta friend said, "Say, I hope you don't have to go, because he's going to come out as soon as the program's over." I found I had a few more minutes, and decided to stay. I looked out the window and saw him drive up in a convertible. He did look even better than he sounded.

I became that friend who was sticking closer than a brother. The four of us, my neighbor, the Atlanta friend, her boyfriend, and I, spent practically the whole weekend together. Sunday night, we took the Atlanta friend to the station to put her on the train back to Atlanta. I thought to myself, "If I walk back to the car faster than my neighbor, I can get in the middle seat." You don't take the person in the middle seat home first. So this boyfriend and I dropped off my neighbor, and that was the beginning of a wonderful friendship between me and this boy who had a radio program.

He was quite a ham. He sang on our every date and I decided that if I was going to be discovered, I would have to sing louder than him. So one night, I tuned up and sang louder than he did. He said, "Hey. That's not bad. You're going to have to come sing on my radio program."

I said, "Who? Little ol' me? When do you want me to come?"

He said, "Maybe next week. How about that?"

I said, "Oh, that would just be great. I could come next week." Next week found me right there, right on key, and I sang on the radio for the first time.

I wasn't a Christian then, so I couldn't even pray about my big chance. But I got through it and a few days later the manager of the radio station called me and said, "We have a new band that's forming in Birmingham. They're auditioning vocalists. Would you like to come down and audition?"

I ran down, I auditioned, and they must have been hard up for singers because I got the job. We had about 350 people coming to the Pickwick Club to hear us. Well, there I was, up on the stage, a band behind me, 30-minute radio program every Sunday afternoon. This was big stuff in Birmingham, Alabama. And I knew that I was well on my way. I knew that one Sunday afternoon, a scout from Hollywood would come through Birmingham and would tune in and say, "What do we have here?" And I would be whisked off to Hollywood and that would be it.

Well, it didn't happen exactly that way, but I can honestly

tell you that after a few months, I began to ask myself the question: "Do you mean this is all there is to having a career?" It became very boring and I knew this wasn't really what I wanted for my life.

Marriage

I think it was then that my thoughts turned toward matrimony: *This is what brings fulfillment in a woman's life — meeting the man of her dreams, and capturing that man, and living happily ever afterwards. That's it. That's what I want.*

So as I began to look around, one night I was at a formal dance. I was standing by a friend up in the balcony, looking down on the dance floor and I saw the best-looking man I had ever seen in my life. I said to her, "Who is that?"

She said, "Oh, that's Captain Bud Newbold. Haven't you met him yet?" This was during the war (the *Second* World War).

I said, "No. But I've waited long enough. You be sure and introduce me tonight before we leave, because that's the man I think I'd like to marry."

Captain Bud Newbold just kept on dancing, not knowing what was going on up in the balcony. But my friend did introduce me to him that night, and after I met him three more times he finally remembered my name. Fortunately, he remembered my phone number, too, because he called and we started dating. Would you believe that six months later he had talked me into marrying him??

After the wedding we moved to St. Petersburg, Florida, and you couldn't have a more beautiful place to begin a marriage. I remember riding down the street one day, pinching myself. Can it be true? I have married the man of my dreams. I live in the place of my dreams. I could fish, I could swim, I could tan, I could play bridge. I could do anything I wanted to do. He drove to Tampa every day and I stayed home, but I had a lot of friends and had more fun being a wife.

Bud and I, who planned to live happily ever after, were as

happy as we could be for about four or five months. And then it began. You see, I had always been the kind of person who believed that there was only one way to do anything and, of course, that was my way. And would you believe that out of this great big world of men, I married a man who was exactly like I was? He knew there was only one way to do things, but it certainly wasn't my way. I was amazed that he could come up with an alternative way every time. Before very long, I began to ask myself the question, *Do you mean this is all there is to a beautiful marriage?*

We began picking at each other.

The Bible says that the wise woman builds her home, the foolish woman plucketh it down with her hands. And I was that foolish woman and began to pluck down my marriage with my own hands. And it wasn't very long until Bud and I didn't even like each other.

Bud came from a family that didn't believe in divorce. I think that's about the only thing that held us together at that particular time. We really hadn't talked about it openly, but we both knew we were headed toward the divorce court.

Well, the war was over, Bud got out of the service, and we decided to move back to the small town in Iowa where Bud had come from. His father was a lawyer, the mayor of the city, head of the school board, head of this, head of that, head of everything there, I think. His mother was the first woman county attorney in Iowa. She was a lawyer, his older brother was a lawyer. Bud said the family thought there was something wrong with you if you didn't turn out to be a lawyer, so he became a lawyer, too. And now he was going back to start his law practice with his mother and father.

I was excited about it. I had heard so much about Pop and Emi, as he called them. Everyone else called his mother "Emily L." And they said of "Emily L" that they would rather look at anybody from the witness stand than Emily L. Newbold. She had eyes that were like steel and she could look right through you.

Well, I didn't know all this. She was Bud's loving mother and that's all I heard from him. I just couldn't wait to meet the family. So we got up there with cold winter snow everywhere.

We didn't even have a heater in the car. They were non-existent during the war. We finally bought one on the way up but we couldn't find anyone to install it. So we got there numb and frozen.

I walked up and the door opened and there was Emily L. I stepped forward and held out my arms. She immediately reached out, took me by the waist, moved me over to one side, and said, *"Bud!"*

The lines were drawn. There wasn't anything she could have done after that to have made me like her. The feeling was mutual. She couldn't stand me from the moment she saw me.

We found out that in this small town there was just a certain number of houses. Somebody had to move out of town before a house became available for newcomers to move in. We were to live in the big house with Bud's parents. So that began our year in Iowa.

Then I *really* asked myself the question: *Do you mean this is all there is to a beautiful marriage?* I thought seriously about going home and even voiced it at one time. It was Bud's father who really kept us together. He was the dearest, sweetest man I have ever known in all my life. He was a delight, the one shining light in my life at that time.

Motherhood

I discovered that we had an addition to the family on the way and I knew *that* was going to do it. A baby. *That's* what a woman's born for! That's what a woman looks forward to, when she shall hold that little baby in her arms. And that little baby is going to draw mother and daddy closer together, and it's going to make the family what you've always wanted it to be. *That's* going to make everything perfect, when the Gerber baby comes.

So I waited for the Gerber baby, sick and miserable the

whole time. But I was going to have a baby. Nobody had ever had a baby in this world but me. Then Susan came and since she was premature, she really looked like my great grandmother instead of the Gerber baby. Her little face was big around with a million wrinkles in it. I knew they had made a mistake right at first, but soon she began to shape up and was the cutest little thing you ever saw.

But along with the baby comes a lot of responsibility. I was haggard and drawn. I knew she couldn't sleep through the night without choking to death or she wouldn't breathe if I didn't go in and watch her every now and then. Bud slept beautifully through the nights. He never heard a sound. He said, years later, "Did Susan ever wake you up at night?"

Through all of this, I began to ask myself the question, *Do you mean this is all there is to beautiful motherhood?* None of these things were bringing the fulfillment for which my heart was longing.

Bud and I had both just about really had it up in Iowa. Even he was feeling the strain between his mother and me. He finally decided he was more of a Southerner than I was. So we moved back to Birmingham.

It's said that God has placed himself, has placed eternity, in our hearts, and our hearts are restless until they rest in Him. But we went to church only one time and that was to have Susan christened. Bud and I grew up in Sunday school and church until the time we got old enough to say, "That's it. That's enough."

I thought there were some Christians who liked church and some Christians who didn't like church. I just happened to be one of those who didn't like church. So when I was old enough to really plant my feet and say, "No," I quit going to church and Sunday school. I *did* go on Easter. I always got myself an outfit for Easter and went to church. But it really didn't mean anything to me.

Elizabeth Newbold

The Search

When Susan was about four years old, I remember riding down the road one day and saw a sign that said, "Don't send your child to Sunday school, take your child to Sunday school." Everything noble in me rose to the surface. I thought, *This is proof. You should be a good example for your children.*

Sunday mornings at our house had been spent reading the Sunday papers and lying in bed and catching up from the parties of the weekend. That was a day of rest. But now I thought, *This is something we need to do. Susan is four years old. They entered me in the cradle roll in Sunday school. It's time for her to be in Sunday school.*

I went home and told Bud what I had seen, and said, "Somebody ought to take Susan to Sunday school so she can learn about God and about Jesus Christ."

He said, "I agree with you. That's right. *You* take her."

So Sunday morning I got dressed, and I picked out the biggest church in Birmingham, because there was nothing too good for our daughter. I dressed her and Bud dropped us off while he went to the office to take care of some work.

We went in and I thought, *I'll sit in with her and bone up a little bit on some of the things that they tell her because she may ask me some questions and I don't remember much about what I learned in Sunday school.*

As I started to take my seat, the teacher said, "Mrs. Newbold, would you mind coming back in about an hour? The children act much better when the parents aren't in here."

I walked out thinking how inconsiderate the church was not to have chairs in the hall for parents to wait in. So I stood around in the hall a few minutes before an attractive looking lady came along and asked, "Are you new here?"

When I said yes, she said, "Would you like to visit my ladies Sunday school class?"

And I told a big, fat, lie, because the last place I wanted to go was a ladies' Sunday school class. But they did have some chairs in there, I knew. So I said, "Yes. That would be great."

I followed her into her Sunday school class and really wasn't prepared for the lovely girl who was teaching that day. My mental picture of a ladies' Sunday school teacher was a sour-faced old lady with oily hair combed back into a tight bun. She would, of course, wear a long black dress and high-top shoes, and carry a huge black Bible.

But Jean Baer was not like that at all. She was just about my age, and someone I could identify with. She was teaching from the Book of Hebrews and tied the Old Testament and the New Testament together. She made it *so interesting!*. I saw that the Bible wasn't just a bunch of isolated books that someone had thrown together, but one story from beginning to end. I thought, *I can't wait until next week to get back and hear some more.*

The next week I got Susan there right on time and into my Sunday school class I went. And each week, I'd go home and tell Bud some of the wonderful things I learned from Jean.

One day, Jean said, "Elizabeth, we have an outstanding Bible teacher who's coming to town. He's going to be here for a week of meetings. I want you and Bud to go on Monday night."

She gave him a big build-up; he was even in "Who's Who of America". I had never heard of a preacher who was in "Who's Who of America." She added, "He speaks in five different languages. He travels all over the world and lectures. He used to be a professor at one of the big eastern universities. And he was married to one of the Tiffany girls of New York."

That convinced me! I thought, *I think I'd pay to see this fellow.* I went home and gave Bud the same big build-up. I had said to Jean, "I'll go, but I know Bud isn't going to go."

She said, "Well, you ask him and I'll pray, okay?"

Now, she did some powerful praying, because after I gave Bud the run-down on this preacher, he said, "Yes, I think I'd like to hear this fellow."

When the night came, we went to hear Dr. Donald Gray Barnhouse. We got there late, thinking we'd sit in the back where we wouldn't be noticed. But the church was already filled up. The ushers were bringing in chairs and putting them right down front. So right in front of this man, we sat.

I wasn't prepared for Dr. Barnhouse. When I *had* attended church, it was one that was rather liberal and didn't have any Bible teaching. So I didn't know anything about the Bible. But this man began to speak that night, and I knew that he knew what he was talking about. I have never heard anyone speak with such authority.

At one point he talked about the fact that Christ was coming again one day. He said, "We know that He will come the second time because there is eight times more prophecy of His second coming than there was of His first coming. And over 300 prophecies were literally fulfilled in this one Man when He came the first time. We don't know when He'll come again, but we are told to look for His imminent return. He could come any moment. He could come tonight. There's no prophecy in the Bible that has to be fulfilled before He comes."

I really started paying attention, because everything in me was saying, "I sure do want to know Him. I sure do want to see Him. I didn't know He was coming again."

Dr. Barnhouse said, "You know, if He should come tonight, every person in this room who has eternal life would be caught up in the air with Him, ever to be with Him throughout eternity."

I thought, *Boy, I sure do hope I have eternal life.*

To my shock, Dr. Barnhouse's next words were, "But if you just hope you have eternal life, you don't have it."

I sat up straight and listened intently for I didn't have eternal life, whatever that was. I always thought eternal life was something you would get when you died if you had been good enough. And God would tack it on so you would keep on living.

Dr. Barnhouse explained the real meaning. He said, "Eternal life is the life of the eternal God himself. It's a different quality of life from human life. Human life has a beginning and it has an ending. God's life, eternal life, has no beginning, and it has no ending. It's a different kind of life. Sometime between the time that I'm born into this world and the time that I die, if I am not born of the life that is God's life, then I don't have the life that can have fellowship with God." I sat utterly amazed.

Dr. Barnhouse gave an example. "I went through an automobile factory not long ago and in one room there was a big pile of scrap metal and a huge arm that came out with a magnet on it. It would pick up the metal and take it away on a conveyor belt to be melted down and used again. I watched it for a while, and noticed that some of the metal was just left lying on the floor. And I said to the guide, 'What's the matter with that metal?' He said, 'Well, you see, sir, to your eye and mine, it all looks like good metal. But that's why we have a magnet instead of a man. This is Imitation metal and there's nothing in it to respond to the magnet.' "

Dr. Barnhouse said, "It would be that way tonight if Christ should come again. You all look like wonderful Christians to me. You're in the place where Christians ordinarily would be, in a church. You may go to church every time the door opens. Maybe you teach a Sunday school class. You might be superintendent of the Sunday school department, you may sing in the choir or play the organ and you're there all the time. On the surface, you may look like a Christian. But if you don't have eternal life, you are an imitation Christian. If Christ should come tonight, there is nothing in you to respond to the life of Christ. You'd be left sitting where you are."

And I had the most awful thought: *Boy, with my luck, He's going to come tonight, and whatever this is you're supposed to have, Dr. Barnhouse said I didn't have it. I bet everybody in this room would go up but me, and I'd be sitting here all by myself —*

and wouldn't that be embarrassing? Then I thought, *No, I'll bet Bud would be here, too.* That was my only comfort. And he would have been there, too.

In closing, that preacher prayed "Lord, if there be one person here who has not been born of Thee and who does not have eternal life, I pray you will accompany them with a spirit of restlessness until they rest in Thee."

I thought, *That's got to be the ugliest prayer I ever heard a preacher pray in all my life,* because I knew who he was praying for. Since then I have thanked God for that prayer many times. Going home that night I was restless. Bud was driving the car, I was sitting in the front with him. Jean was in the back seat with a friend of hers. I thought, *I have to keep this casual. I don't want anybody to know how little I know.*

But I turned to Jean, and I said, "Jean, what was he talking about tonight when he said you had to be born again? I never have liked that phrase. Is that just a figure of speech, or is that a reality?"

She said, "No, Elizabeth. That's a reality. You see, that's what makes a Christian different from everybody else in the world. A Christian has been born twice. Once of human life, and once of life from above, spiritual life."

I said, "Is this what he was talking about 'eternal life'?"

"That's right"

"Well, he said that that was a gift. How do you get it, Jean?"

She said, "You receive it, and you say, 'Thank you.' You trust Christ as your personal Savior."

I said, "Aw, Jean, I've heard that all my life. I trust God. I try to trust. What do you do? Nothing happens to me."

She said, "Do you believe that Christ died for your sins?"

I said, "Well, of course. I'm knowledgeable. He died for the sins of the world." Did she think I hadn't even been to the Easter program?

She said, "No. That's not exactly what I mean, Elizabeth.

I mean, do you believe that Jesus, when He died on the cross, died in your place to pay the penalty for your sin? Do you believe that He has already paid the penalty for all of your sin — past sins, present sins, any future sin that you will ever commit? Do you believe that He has paid for all of it and God has nothing against you?"

I said, "Jean, do you mean to tell me that that man dying nearly 2,000 years ago had something to do with my sin?"

She said, "He had everything to do with it, Elizabeth. He either paid for all of it — every bit of it — or you will spend an eternity paying for it, separated from God. That's the penalty."

For the first time in my life, it all fit together. Almost. I said, "Jean, that's the most exciting thing I've ever heard. That's the best news I've ever heard."

She said, "Well, that's what the gospel is. In the Greek, it means, 'good news.' "

Memories of Sunday school flashed through my mind. All I had ever heard was the bad news. "Here are the 10 Commandments. Now, Elizabeth, memorize the 10 Commandments." Oh, I had no problem with that. I memorized the 10 Commandments, got a button for it. Then I was told, "Keep the 10 Commandments. If you keep the 10 Commandments, you'll probably go to heaven when you die." That's all that ever got through to me and that's all I ever understood. And believe me, that *was* the bad news.

What a relief to hear the Good News that night. The first thing I heard was that whatever it took for me to live with God eternally, I didn't have it. And the next thing was that there was created in my heart a desire to know Him and to have this life eternal.

So I said to her, "Jean, I'm not going to promise you that I'm going to be a Christian, though, because I've tried to live the Christian life and all I've ever done is failed."

She said, "Yes, Elizabeth. This is all you will ever do — fail. You see, you've been trying to live the Christian life without the life of Christ in you to give you the power. You know, Elizabeth, there's only one person in the universe who can live the Christian life and that's Jesus Christ. And He's on the outside of your life. But He says, 'Behold, I stand at the door and knock. If any man hear my voice and open the door, I will come into him.' "

She continued, "He wants to come in and be the enabling power for you to live the kind of life you've always wanted to live but couldn't."

Then it really made sense. Very quietly that night, without an outward prayer, I thanked the Lord that He had died for me and paid for all my sins, and I asked Him to come into my heart, and He heard me and He came in that night.

Bud didn't say a single word, but he heard everything I did. That night he asked Christ to come into his life. We got to Jean's home, and when she got out of the car, she gave us two little books. I'll never forget the name of my book — *Regeneration: The Inescapable Imperative.*

We got into bed and I couldn't wait to start reading. I said, "Hey Bud, listen to this. Have you ever heard this before in your life?" And I read to him from my book. He said, "No I never heard that before, but listen to this." And he read to me from his book. And we began that wonderful adventure of the new discoveries that every Christian makes.

We had been two independent people, going our own independent ways. Miles apart. We put our eyes on Christ, and began to learn about Him. And we began to be excited about Him and went to every Bible class we could find. We bought a new Bible, and read Christian books and learned more about Christ. And as we got closer to Christ, we looked around one day, and we were close together! God put our marriage back together in the most beautiful way. I can't think of anybody in the world who has a more wonderful marriage than Bud and I. And, boy, the Lord brought us from way out in left field. He really did.

I have found that Christ is sufficient for every need in our life. I told you about my mother-in-law. You see, I didn't just have a mother-in-law. I had a county attorney. But after Christ came into our lives, He began to mend that relationship. Before she died, she and I had become good friends. We really liked and admired one another. God is sufficient for even mother-in-law problems.

Commitment

After about five years of going to Bible studies, Jean said to me, "I want you to go with me to a Bible conference up in Ashville, North Carolina."

I didn't say it to Jean, but I thought, *I don't want to get that close to those* dedicated *Christians.* Now, up until that time, I wanted to listen to Bible classes but I still wanted the world. I was a fence straddler. I wanted the best of the Christian life and the best of the world which made me a miserable Christian.

Jean wanted me to go to this Bible conference and she and the Lord hemmed me in. She countered all my excuses until I finally agreed to go. I had been hearing a lot of messages about a total surrender of your life to Christ in order that He might make known His will for your life. I would always think, *But how do I know* His *will is what* my *will is? I'll bet that as soon as I surrender my life to Him, He'll send me off to Africa as a missionary!*

Africa was at the bottom of my list of places that I wanted to go. I knew that He would take me away from my husband and my baby, and send me off to Africa with that big black Book to sit on a river bank somewhere and tell the naked natives how they could become Christians. So I would hold on to my seat.

But oh, boy, the voice of God was strong. When I got to the Bible conference, there was a missionary hour at 11 o'clock. Suddenly I felt ill. I said to Jean, "I don't feel very well. I think I'll go rest this period." She said, "No. You don't rest when you come up here. You go to every meeting."

Elizabeth Newbold

I found myself every day at 11 o'clock sitting there listening to two women missionaries from *guess where*? Doesn't God have a marvelous sense of humor? These two woman told how God had spared their lives in the most unbelievable circumstances. They weren't afraid of anything. And I found myself saying to the Lord, "Lord, why are they not afraid of anything? They are Christians. I'm a Christian. I live in a civilized country; I'm afraid to drive downtown at night by myself. What's the difference?"

It seemed the Lord said to me, "Would you do what they've done?" And I thought, *See there! Give Him an inch and He'll take a mile; I knew it!*

But I said, "Lord, no. I don't want to go to Africa as a missionary." Then the Holy Spirit began to bring to my mind the things I had been hearing that week: "Don't you know that if you've been joined to Christ, you've been joined into His death and into His resurrection?"

I began to get the picture that for a Christian we really do go down in death with Christ. But that's not all. We don't stay there. We are raised in newness of life that Christ might live His life through us again. It's like a truck ran over me when I came to Christ that day. And my life ended. All of my plans, all of my dreams, it's as though they ended. I belong to Christ. He bought me at a tremendous cost that He might live in my life, live *His* life over again down here and reach through my life to others. Draw them into His kingdom, build them up in His likeness and send them forth. That's it. That's the Christian life. I said, "Lord, if Africa is where you want me, I know that I could never know fulfillment anywhere else in the world and if that's what you want of me, that's where I want to go."

The next day, there was an altar call for people who were willing to go into missions. I was ready. I hopped up and started to go down, and the speaker said, "That is, all of you that are 30 years old or younger." I was 40 and I couldn't get

into the age group. On the way home I prayed, "Lord, open doors of service for me." I added a little addendum to my prayer. I said, "Lord, and when you open the door, would you push me through it? Because I won't go if you don't." And He's been pushing me through them ever since then, so wonderfully, so gently, and life has been so exciting!

The Call

Later that year, Bud and Elizabeth attended a church in their new neighborhood. The president of the married couples' Sunday school class came up to Elizabeth and asked her to give the opening devotional the next week.

"Why, I can't do that," Elizabeth stammered. She felt the blood drain from her face, Just the thought of standing up in front of people and "preaching" left her knees weak.

Suddenly Bud stood by her elbow. "This is the strangest thing," he said. "You claim to have given your life to the Lord. You've even promised to do anything He wants you to do or say what He wants you to say. Yet the first time he opens a door of opportunity to speak for Him, you say no."

Elizabeth glared at Bud. This wasn't what she had in mind. She meant that she would be willing to face lions, snakes, or wild men in Africa — but never to stand up in front of 80 people in Sunday school and speak! That was impossible!

The next week, sitting next to Bud in the class, she prayed desperately, "Lord, I don't know why you put me in this situation, but all I ask is that you keep me from fainting in front of all these people."

The moment arrived.

Elizabeth walked to the podium and gripped it so hard her knuckles turned white. Her lips trembled and turned purple — even through her lipstick! Her hand shook as she turned the pages of her Bible.

To her relief, her knees held her up through the five minutes she spoke. Wet with perspiration she sat down and glanced at Bud for reassurance. He smiled.

Elizabeth Newbold

After church she and Bud sat in the car and laughed. Then Elizabeth confided to him, "You know what? It just dawned on me that God answered my prayer. He kept me standing up, and that's all I asked. Next time, I'll ask Him for everything I need — including something to say the next time I'm asked to speak. If I ask for little things, I'll get little things. If I ask for bigger things, God will give accordingly."

Little did Elizabeth know that "bigger things" — much bigger in fact — were coming her way. Doors she never knew existed would soon begin to open up.

The Messenger

God took Elizabeth's commitment seriously, but He didn't send her to Africa. He called her first to the heathen in America, and to do the thing she feared most — speaking to groups of people.

God brought a spiritual renewal to Birmingham. And the person He chose to turn the hearts of so many people back to the Lord was dynamic, intelligent Elizabeth Newbold. She stood in the gap and made the way of salvation clear to thousands.

It began with the youth group in her church. And more and more teenagers responded to her enthusiasm about the Bible. Then it spread as Elizabeth and four of her friends started meeting together for Bible study and prayer. The group grew from five to ten, and in six months they had outgrown the living room where they were meeting.

The class was split into two different groups under Elizabeth's teaching, but within a year both groups outgrew the homes. They then moved the study to a local city hall building where they could fit everyone in.

The first time Janie Buck attended the study, the group had been forced to temporarily move downstairs in the city hall building because of renovation. In her book, she recalls:

> *I found the stairs and shivered when my hand touched the metal stair rail. The cement floor of the*

177

basement was damp. The pipes overhead sputtered. The gray cinder block walls made the place even gloomier. I sat in a rusty folding chair near the back, amazed to find the room filled with women.

In front of the room, standing by a small lectern, was the most radiantly alive person I had ever seen. Elizabeth taught a lesson unlike anything I had ever heard. She made practical applications showing how God intended us to live. Even the way she read the Bible was different. It sounded as if she had written it herself.

I felt the sunshine had been turned on in my soul. The dreary basement faded as I basked in the love of God. Elizabeth lifted up and magnified the Lord Jesus. A deep hunger in my heart was satisfied. The cloud that usually hung over me melted like the fog in the valley in front of my house. I had found what I was looking for even though I couldn't have put my finger on what I needed. My restlessness was satisfied, for here was someone who could teach me how to apply the Bible to my life.

It amazed Elizabeth to see not only the number of women but also the social levels represented among them. Many socially and financially prominent women found their lives revolutionized. Conversation at the country clubs ran less and less to gossip and more and more to the gospel and who became a Christian that week.

God was about to expand Elizabeth's sphere of influence.

In 1961, the Communists created an international crisis in building their infamous wall around East Berlin. The U.S. government federalized national guard units including the Alabama Air National Guard, in which Bud Newbold served as a colonel. His unit was called to active duty and sent to France. Elizabeth and their daughter Susan stayed behind the first

Elizabeth Newbold

month, until Bud called and told them he wanted them to join him. Encouraging the women in the Bible study to continue studying for themselves, Elizabeth boarded the Queen Mary with her daughter on December 7 and sailed for France.

During their time in France, Elizabeth not only impacted a number of men and women at the base, but she and Bud also renewed a friendship with the man who was head of International Christian Leadership, Wallace Hanes. Through that association, Elizabeth found herself facing one of the most exciting challenges yet.

Every year, Wallace Hanes traveled to Finland to encourage the Bible classes that had been organized by a couple who lived there. But that year his schedule was too hectic to accommodate the trip. Knowing something of Elizabeth and her teaching ability, he asked her to go in his place.

God worked out the necessary details, and Elizabeth found herself in Finland teaching the Bible and sharing her testimony with people of nobility, highly educated world leaders, and the leading economists, scientists, and businessmen in the country.

"Lord," she prayed, "what am I trying to do? I don't know anything about economics. I don't know anything about running governments."

God answered by bringing to mind I Corinthians 2 where Paul said he "determined to know nothing among you except Jesus Christ, and Him crucified." That settled what she would talk about.

She first addressed a Bible study at the request of Baroness Jeanne Marie Von Korring, who became a close friend. The next day was a gathering at the home of Viljo Castren, a professor at the University of Helsinki whose research had been honored by the Massachusetts Institute of Technology. Elizabeth proclaimed Christ before ministers in the Finnish cabinet, delegates to the United Nations, and members of the Finnish Parliament. And everywhere she went, the response was so great that those who

179

heard her speak extended still more invitations for additional speaking engagements.

Before leaving, she confided to the baroness, "You know, Jeanne Marie, I'm praying that those who hear me teach will confront Jesus directly and say either 'yes' or 'no' to Him. One of my constant prayers is that the Lord will make me a fork in the road, so those who listen to me will either turn to Him or at least know they have consciously chosen not to turn to Him. If I leave people simply drifting along in blind indifference, I fail them and God."

Baroness Von Korring replied, "That's what makes you so different, Elizabeth. You radiate such a strong sense of mission, of destiny, of purpose. I'm praying your sense of purpose and even your communication skills will rub off on me."

After returning to France, Bud and Elizabeth again visited with Wallace Hanes. He showed them a letter he had received from Dr. Virkkunen, one of the leading theologians of Finland, who had been intrigued by Elizabeth's presentation of the gospel and the meaning of being born again.

Of Elizabeth, this very important and intelligent man had written that he had never met anyone, man or woman, who taught the Bible with such clarity. It was quite an exciting adventure for this housewife from Birmingham.

By the end of August 1961 the crisis created by the Russian blockade of Berlin simmered down, and the Newbolds returned home. The phone lines hummed in Birmingham. Elizabeth was home! The Bible class resumed, and at the first meeting, the City Hall overflowed.

Over time, a number of women petitioned Elizabeth to begin an evening class so their husbands could come and hear the things they had been learning. Twelve people attended the first night class in the living room of one of the couples. Within a few months, all 20 seats in the sunken living room were filled, and a row of chairs had to be set up on the upper level. Before long, a second row of chairs had to be added.

Elizabeth Newbold

Eventually a policeman was hired to help with the parking problem, and within two years the class had swelled to 150 people. There was a nucleus of "regulars" who came each week, but many, many people came to see and hear the lady who had changed their friends' lives. Hundreds trusted Christ.

The requests for Elizabeth's teaching continued to pour in, and before long, she was teaching Bible studies in Atlanta, Tuscaloosa, and Huntsville, as well as Birmingham.

But there was a price to pay. Elizabeth's daughter Susan had come to bitterly resent the time and effort her mother had poured into teaching and counseling. After attending a Bill Gothard Seminar and learning that Christian workers should put their families before their ministry, Elizabeth apologized to Susan and asked forgiveness for not putting her first. In her testimony, Elizabeth talked about the daughter who almost broke her heart:

I have learned that Christ is sufficient for rebellious children. Our daughter was very rebellious. I didn't know it, but a seed of resentment, a seed of bitterness, was sown in her heart at an early age because her mother was so busy teaching Bible classes. I never felt that I had neglected her. My mother was always there and she adored Susan, but that's not like her own mother. Susan grew up with this bitterness festering in her and the bitterness toward me was projected toward God. By the time she was in high school and into college, she would say, "Don't talk to me about that stuff."

She married and had a child. One day, when her health was just about broken, she said to me, "The doctor suggested I go to a psychiatrist." I said, "Honey, you don't need to go to a psychiatrist. You've just got one problem. You hate your mama. I made so many mistakes in the very beginning. We didn't have all these wonderful family life conferences and all of that, no guidelines. And I made a lot of mistakes. I have asked you to forgive me, and I can't go back and change the past."

And Susan said, "I will never forgive you!"

That just absolutely stabbed me through the heart, but I said to her, "Well, darlin', you've got a problem. I've asked God to forgive me and He has forgiven me. But it's going to eat you up inside if you don't forgive me. You see, I've become your emotional focus. Whatever you hate is your emotional focus as much as what you love. And whatever your emotional focus is, you become just like it. In other words, darlin', you're going to be just like your mother."

"Where does it say that?" Susan questioned.

We went over some things that Bill Gothard had had to say about bitterness, and I left her to think about that. Susan went back home to Tuscaloosa and called two days later. She said, "Mother, can you ever forgive me? God has. I prayed and I invited Him into my heart. He's there. I've been born again. I read that Bible you gave me, I hadn't even opened it before, and I read until 4:30 this morning. I want you to know that I love you."

That was just about the second greatest day in all of my life. Susan was born again running. She goes everywhere now to share her testimony of what Christ means to her and what He has done in her life.

In the coming months and years, Susan and Elizabeth became best friends. Susan even inherited her mother's ability to speak and present the Lord in such an effective way that hundreds of women come to Christ each year through her testimony. She always tells about her rebellion against her parents. She has said, "My mother was an overcomer. She didn't let a rebellious daughter stop her from obeying the Lord."

In reflecting on her relationship with her daughter, Elizabeth stated:

Christ is sufficient for young people who have turned their back on everything that you've taught them and everything that you want them to know. Rebellious teenagers, rebellious young adults, He is sufficient to mend that situation and make it right.

Harvesting

Through a series of events, God eventually led Bud and Elizabeth to join the staff of Campus Crusade for Christ and they were assigned to work in Asia. During the next nine years, their lives would be poured out in places like Iran, Cambodia, Laos, Singapore, Korea, Japan, their home base in the Philippines, and even as far as Australia. They proclaimed Christ before Communists, Muslims, Buddhists, and atheists. Their straightforward presentation of the gospel, accompanied by their genuine love for the lost, was embraced by thousands. Everywhere they traveled they found people who were eager to surrender their lives to the Savior who was so joyfully and lovingly introduced to them.

It seemed that no one escaped Elizabeth's watchful eye. In addition to formally addressing thousands of people through Campus Crusade conferences, she looked for every opportunity to share the news about Jesus Christ one on one with people who crossed her path. Using Campus Crusades' "Four Spiritual Laws" booklet as a guide, she witnessed to taxi drivers, college students, bellboys, soldiers, a Buddhist Temple guide, and even a young girl being kept as a slave in a house of prostitution on the island of Fiji.

It happened as Elizabeth was wandering through neighborhoods one day as part of a witnessing program. She stumbled upon a young girl in a flowered dress who was sitting on the railing of an upstairs balcony. Eager to share with her, she followed as the girl motioned to "come with me." They came to a door which was made of heavy iron, like a jailhouse door! It was locked from the inside. Suddenly Elizabeth knew the girl's occupation. A flashback from a newspaper article about white slavery rackets in Fiji sprang alarmingly into Elizabeth's mind.

An enormous man opened the door with a key he took from his pocket and stared out at them. He was stripped to the waist

and barefooted, like the girl. Elizabeth glanced in and saw two more big men playing pool in the dimly lit room.

She prayed silently, "Lord, if they intend to harm me, I'll never get down all those steps in time to get away, so I trust you to protect me."

Then the Lord gave her a calming thought, "In nothing be terrified by your adversaries." And she did have one thing going for her. Never had she been more happy to be nearing 60!

Elizabeth followed the sullen young woman to another door and into a room where six girls were sitting on the floor eating. Their hands stopped halfway to their mouths as they gaped at Elizabeth.

The girl from the front porch stood to one side, leering sarcastically at Elizabeth as if to say, "Now what was it you wanted to ask?"

Elizabeth recovered her composure and began to question the girls. None of them responded except a brown-skinned girl sitting in the corner who nodded her head with just a hint of sympathy for Elizabeth's predicament.

As the other girls became bored and left the room, Elizabeth shared the Four Spiritual Laws booklet with the young girl. When she read Law Three, "God's only provision for man's sin is Jesus Christ; through Him you can know God's love and forgiveness," she looked up and saw big tears rolling down the girl's cheeks.

"Ma'am. do you mean that God would have anything to do with me?"

"Oh, my goodness yes!" Elizabeth said. "He loves you. My prayer to God this morning was that He would lead me to someone on this island whose heart He had prepared and who really wanted to know Him. I didn't want to waste my time talking to people who are not interested. I just asked Him specifically to lead me to those who are. You weren't very easy to find, either. I had to come through that locked door to get to you."

With that, the girl really began to cry. She had to mop her eyes to read the fourth law. Then she prayed to receive Christ and her face glowed with joy through tears.

Elizabeth made sure the girl understood what she had done and told her how to grow as a new Christian. Inwardly she groaned at having to leave her in that place. Never had it been so difficult to leave someone who had prayed with her to receive Christ.

The girl escorted her to the front door. The burly door-keeper opened it without a word. Elizabeth looked longingly at the teary-eyed girl and motioned for her to follow, but she shook her head sadly.

Back at the church, Elizabeth talked to the Christians about the girl. They said it was impossible to rescue women in those houses. Still, the whole church prayed that God would close up the houses and help them win the hearts of the people inside.

Bud and Elizabeth left Fiji, but sometime later they were relating the story of the young girl to a fellow missionary who was then assigned to Fiji.

He sat in silent amazement. "Do you know what that house is?" he asked.

"I didn't know when I went up the steps, but I quickly realized it was a house of prostitution," Elizabeth answered.

"No, I don't mean then. Do you know what that house is NOW?"

"No, what is it?"

"It's the new headquarters for Campus Crusade for Christ in Fiji!"

The missionary then related how the run-down area had been so affected by people's response to the gospel that even the police wanted to know what was going on that was making such a difference. The Christians finally addressed the policemen as a group and many of them prayed to receive Christ, and even enrolled in a special class to learn how to lead others to Christ. This dynamic group of policemen regularly went out to share their faith with people on the island.

Secrets of a Fulfilled Woman

Elizabeth rejoiced. She said, "If God could use me, He will use anybody!"

Sufficient Grace

After two fruitful years in Asia, Bud and Elizabeth returned home on a three-month furlough. It was then that Elizabeth was confronted with an entirely different kind of challenge. She later recalled the following.

I used to wonder as I counseled so many women in my Bible classes, many of whom would tell me that they had cancer. And they would come to me absolutely distraught and say, "Elizabeth, what in the world am I going to do?" I could open the Bible and show them in the Bible what God had said; I could tell them where they could find peace. But I used to wonder to myself: "What would I do if the doctor told me that I had cancer?"

Well, I was to find that out after we had been in Asia for two years. The first time we came home, Bud had to have a hernia operation. He had carried my bags all over Asia and used to kid me and say the big one was my cosmetic bag. But we would be gone for six weeks or two months at a time, and to all kinds of climates, so we had to take *everything* with us. When he went to the doctor for a checkup, the doctor said, "Not one hernia, but two." After his operation we went to Florida for him to recuperate.

We hurried back so I could run by and see the doctor for a checkup. He examined me and said, "You're going to think I'm working for the hospital, but you've got to go to the hospital, too. You've got a lump in your breast. What's your schedule?" I told him, and he said, "Cancel it for the next month." I said, "You haven't even done a biopsy yet." He said, "I don't have to, I know what it is. It's cancer."

You know, the Lord is our shepherd when we commit our lives to Him. He leads us, and had been leading me for quite some time. He prepares us for what is ahead. Christ is the only

Elizabeth Newbold

One who can see around the curve of my life. I don't know what's down there until I get there. But He has promised me that if I will walk with Him, then He will prepare me for everything that lies ahead. Honestly, my reaction when the doctor told me that I had cancer — and it's all because of how Christ had prepared me for such a moment — was, "Isn't this exciting!"

Some people might say I needed to have my head examined, but that's exactly the way I felt about it. I thought, *This can only go two ways. Either He's going to take me home to be with Him and wouldn't that be exciting! Or, I'm going to go through an exciting experience with Jesus Christ down here that I've never been through before and I've never gotten to know Him in the way I'll know Him now.*

It takes God to do that kind of a miracle. And I want to say that He was absolutely sufficient. There never has been a time when I have known fear because of my cancer. There have been some unpleasant times in it. That's when I draw closer to the Lord than at any other time. I know there probably will be some unpleasant times ahead of me as I face what's out there. But He has promised me one thing and I believe Him: "My grace is sufficient for you." Not grace today to think about two weeks ahead of time, and what's going to happen down the road or two months or two years from now. But grace for right now, for this day. He has been teaching me how to live one day at a time. Not living in the past: "Oh, how great it was back there." Not living in the future: "Oh, how wonderful it's going to be when such-and-such occurs." But, "It's today, Lord. What a wonderful day to be alive and to be with You and thank You, Lord, Your grace is sufficient today."

Going Home

Almost five years after her first operation, Elizabeth's cancer returned. She came back to the United States for X-rays and chemotherapy, and again, the cancer went into remission. Bud and Elizabeth returned to the mission field and spent another two years in Asia. Then the cancer came back for the third time, and the Newbolds were re-assigned to Houston, Texas.

Elizabeth received cancer treatment at M. D. Anderson Hospital, while continuing to teach Bible classes and ministering to other patients. After she finished the treatments, she and Bud moved back to their home in Birmingham. Many times during those nine years in Asia she had longed for her former life back in peaceful Birmingham.

She was well enough to teach three Bible classes a week, and she addressed the ladies in her group: "I don't know for sure if the cancer is completely gone or not. But I am absolutely sure I am in the center of God's will. Whether I have cancer or don't have cancer is no longer my main concern. I have given my life and my body to Christ. Since 1956, I have never consciously taken it back. I was so excited when I first learned Christ really meant He wanted to live His life again through me. I knew if I would just believe Him, He would."

A few weeks later Elizabeth was hospitalized again with intense pain in the lower abdomen. When she recovered, she continued speaking again to many groups every week. Few suspected she was sick, for she was radiant and beautiful as ever.

She told another class, "The Great Shepherd of the sheep is perfecting me. Even though I come from a long line of worriers, I am free from worry. I have found a deep settled joy and peace walking with my Lord. Fear of death is behind me now. God is leading me, protecting me, and providing for me. How can I be afraid?"

She went into the hospital again with intense pain caused by a tumor that was blocking the urethra. Again she came through the operation successfully, and the doctor told her she could go home the next day.

"I'm so glad," she told the doctor, who happened to be Jewish. "With Thanksgiving a day away, I want so much to be home with Bud." Then she looked her doctor straight in the eye, took his hand and said, "Thank you, doctor. I want to say goodbye."

Elizabeth Newbold

He was profoundly affected, for later he told one of her good friends, "Elizabeth told me the gospel but she also really loved me. I will never forget her saying 'goodbye.' So many Christians have tried to preach to me, but she loved me."

The next morning Elizabeth dressed, put on her make-up and got back in bed to wait for Bud to come check her out of the hospital.

A coughing spasm hit her and she pushed the call button for the nurse. The nurse hurried in.

"I think you had better call Bud," Elizabeth said.

The nurse sent a Code Blue alarm.

Elizabeth was rushed to intensive care where a team of doctors worked frantically to save her life. In spite of their efforts, a massive blood clot went straight to her lungs and killed her as quickly as if a bolt of lightning had struck her.

Her long time friend and doctor who had first found the cancer came out of the room and found himself face to face with Bud, who had just arrived with their pastor.

"Bud, I told her she could go home today," he said, "but God decided it was time to take her to her true home — heaven."

Estimates of the number of people who attended Elizabeth's funeral ranged from 500 to 900. Midway through the service, their pastor, Dr. Frank Barker, stopped and asked, "By the way, how many here today were led to the Lord by Elizabeth?" Over half the people raised their hands. And most of those were people she had witnessed to before 1971 when she and Bud left to spend nine years in Asia.

Then at the grave site Dr. Barker told a story that really summed up her life. He said, "I had a conversation just this morning with one of the elders of my church. The elder said that he and his wife and two children were having breakfast and the young daughter said, 'I know there will be rejoicing in heaven today because Elizabeth is there.' Whereupon her young brother replied, 'There sure is going to be a lot of rejoicing in hell too because they got that woman off the streets."

Secrets of a Fulfilled Woman

Elizabeth started her ministry for Jesus Christ trembling as she gave her first devotion in Sunday school and ended with her heart full of praises to God! She had seen thousands trust Christ as their Savior, have their lives changed, and their families restored. Hundreds of her disciples were in full-time service for Christ.

In the conclusion of her testimony, Elizabeth talked about the One she had so faithfully served:

"He is sufficient for cancer. I have found Him sufficient for rebellious children. I have found Him sufficient for in-law problems. I have found Him sufficient for a broken marriage. What more could you ask from a Savior?"

To obtain a copy of *Elizabeth: A Blessing to All Nations,* contact Janie Buck, 2409 Vestavia Drive, Birmingham, Alabama 35216 / 205-979-2296.